the whole smiths
real food every day

HEALTHY RECIPES
TO KEEP YOUR FAMILY HAPPY
THROUGHOUT THE WEEK

the whole smiths
real food every day

MICHELLE SMITH

HOUGHTON MIFFLIN HARCOURT

Boston New York 2020

Library of Congress Cataloging-in-Publication Data

Names: Smith, Michelle,
1980– author.

Title: The Whole Smiths real
food every day : healthy recipes
to keep your family happy
throughout the week / Michelle
Smith.

Other titles: Real food every day |
Whole Smiths.

Description: Boston : Houghton
Mifflin Harcourt, 2020. | Includes
index.

Identifiers: LCCN 2020016341
(print) | LCCN 2020016342
(ebook) | ISBN 9780358164463
(paper over board) | ISBN
9780358164517 (ebook)

Subjects: LCSH: Quick and easy
cooking. | Make-ahead cooking. |
LCGFT: Cookbooks.

Classification: LCC TX833.5
.S6436 2020 (print) |
LCC TX833.5 (ebook) |
DDC 641.5/12—dc23

LC record available at https://
lccn.loc.gov/2020016341

LC ebook record available at
https://lccn.loc.gov/2020016342

Book design by Toni Tajima

Printed in China
SCP 10 9 8 7 6 5 4 3 2 1

To Brad,
the hunkiest dishwasher
a girl could ask for

CONTENTS

INTRODUCTION · 1   ABOUT THIS BOOK · 3
FOOD PHILOSOPHY · 5   MEET THE SMITHS · 7
26 KITCHEN HACKS, TIPS, AND TRICKS TO
MAKE YOUR COOKING LIFE EASIER · 9

chapter 1
make ahead, keep on hand *12*

chapter 2
get set, meal prep! *36*

chapter 3
aww, sheet *60*

chapter 4
five ingredients or less *86*

chapter 5
one-dish wonders *116*

chapter 6
30 minutes or less *144*

chapter 7
in an instant *176*

chapter 8
leftovers again? *200*

chapter 9
weekend living *220*

ACKNOWLEDGMENTS · 257
DIETARY CHART · 258   INDEX · 260

INTRODUCTION

If you've picked up this book, it's safe to say you're interested in cooking, healthy food, feeding your loved ones, or all of the above. Or maybe you think healthy eating is for the birds, but a friend gifted it to you and you feel obliged to at least flip through it.

Either way, you're in the right place, and I'm happy you're here.

For the majority of us, eating healthy can oftentimes feel pretentious and unapproachable. We're bombarded with images that portray highly regimented, restrictive lifestyles, leading us to think that the road to health and wellness is through six-pack abs, calorie counting, and a raw-food diet. While all those can be part of a healthier way to eat and live, they don't resonate with most of us, who are simply looking for vitality and balance, and for a way to be healthy without being extreme.

You can still enjoy your favorite foods while living a very healthy lifestyle. In fact, I venture to say, an even healthier lifestyle, because you can release the mental traps that come with the extremes. There's a wide array of "healthy" that falls between a strict one-thousand-calorie-a-day diet designed to maintain a certain size and continually consuming processed fast foods and shot-gunning sugar-laden sodas.

This book represents *that* healthy. The healthy that still loves to have pizza every now and again but is mindful of how it affects your body. The healthy that is more than happy to sneak some of your kids' Halloween candy but knows better than to stock it in the pantry year-round. The healthy that knows it isn't just about a clothing size or the numbers on a scale. The healthy that enjoys an outdoor run but isn't training for an Ironman. The healthy that loves food and doesn't want to give it all up.

If that sounds like you, you're in the right place.

It's time to get back in the kitchen and fall in love with real, whole, delicious foods all over again.

xoxo,
michelle

ABOUT THIS BOOK

I created this book with *you* in mind. The home cook, student, mother, plumber, or dog walker who's interested in feeling good and eating well. Chances are, you have a bustling life and don't have hours to spend in the kitchen chopping, canning, and butchering each and every day.

I get that. Neither do I.

I want to bust the myth that eating well and fueling your body needs to be a time-consuming, laborious, over-the-top process full of hard-to-source items you may never have heard of. You don't need to be a classically trained chef to cook delicious meals on the regular, and you don't need to live next door to a specialty grocery store to make it happen.

My job is to get you into the kitchen and cooking whole-food meals for yourself and your loved ones in an easy and approachable manner. To do this, I want to provide you with simple recipes that use foods and techniques you're familiar with.

Each chapter is dedicated to a mode of cooking or a method of keeping things easy in the kitchen. I've consciously kept the cooking techniques simple and the ingredients easy to find. Some of the concepts may be new to you, but they are by no means difficult to master or inaccessible.

The recipes in this book are composed of whole, minimally processed foods. They aren't loaded with grains, dairy, sugar, or soy, although they may use these ingredients sparingly.

While a few ingredients, like coconut aminos and collagen peptides, may not be found in every grocery store, they're easy to find online, and you can usually have them on your doorstep in two days. In the event you can't find an ingredient or are looking for a swap to accommodate a food allergy or preference, I've also given simple substitutes for ingredients throughout the book. (Please note that I use kosher salt and salted butter in all the recipes here, unless otherwise noted.)

The majority of these recipes are designed to feed four to six people, with the hope that you will have leftovers available for lunch for the next day or two. Portion sizes are hard to determine because everyone is different in their dietary needs. The four to six portions represent an average. How far a recipe stretches for you and your football-playing teenagers is going to vary wildly from how far it stretches for me and my elementary schoolers.

Each recipe indicates the dietary guidelines it follows, such as Paleo, gluten-free, and so on, or can be made to follow with reasonable substitutions, so you can make the recipe or skip it based on your personal food preferences. At the end of the book, the index lets you quickly browse to see which of the recipes fall into each category.

And finally, I've indicated which of the recipes make for exceptionally delicious leftovers. That means they reheat well and taste just as delicious (if not better) the next day.

Like I said, this cookbook was designed for *you*. The greatest compliment I can receive is that the recipes in this book inspired you to get in the kitchen and cook delicious, healthy foods for yourself and your loved ones.

FOOD PHILOSOPHY

Here at The Whole Smiths, we don't label ourselves based on the kinds of food we eat. We're not Paleo or keto or any of the names that have been created for diets that we try to adhere to. We're human beings. And chances are, you are too. (If not, call me. I'm dying to find out more!)

While those labels can work for food, they aren't great for people. Our relationships with food, variations in dietary needs for different individuals, and the cultural ties we have to foods are far too complex for a label.

If you press me to describe our food ideology, I'd say that day to day, we eat high-quality animal proteins, lots of produce, and minimally processed foods. We incorporate quality dairy products and gluten-free grains into our meals, but not on a regular basis. While I'm gluten-intolerant and avoid all gluten, the rest of my family eats it sparingly.

With that said, we'll also dive into some froyo after a soccer game and have pizza on Friday nights when I don't feel like cooking. Not because it's a "cheat day," but because we're human beings, and these things are fun and delicious.

Here's the thing, though: Pizza and froyo don't make up our all-day, every-day diet. We eat plenty of nutrient-dense whole foods throughout the week so we can fully enjoy and appreciate the times when we don't.

I believe we've all outgrown stringent dietary labels. At the end of the day, we just need to know how to cook and shop for whole, minimally processed, nutrient-dense foods. To do that, we need to educate ourselves on the kinds of food products we're eating and get back into the kitchen.

Wellness begins with real food, not the processed, food-like products we've come to accept as food.

MEET THE SMITHS

In the Beginning

Brad and I began dating when "TiK ToK" by Kesha and "California Gurls" by Katy Perry were topping the charts. Our very first date was at a San Jose taqueria where we bonded over our love of their chips and salsa and our disdain for their customer service. Shortly thereafter, we married and started our little family. We've been best friends and partners in life ever since.

Our Journey into Food

After our children were born, I became more and more interested in learning about the foods we were eating. With so much information out there, it's hard to know what is *indeed* healthy. After much research, I discovered the Paleo diet, and we started following dietary parameters similar to those. We weren't rigid with our choices, but simply used the pillars of Paleo to guide our dietary choices.

Paleo seemed like a reasonable fit, as it appeared to be most aligned with how our bodies have evolved to process food—*real* food. I flourished eating whole, minimally processed foods. Things like allergies and skin ailments resolved, and for the first time in a long time, I felt good.

I became really excited about what I was learning about food and wanted to share how we as a growing family were incorporating whole foods into our diets in a manageable, approachable, and fun way. Blogging was becoming popular, and I decided to go for it. I began sharing the new foods we were trying and the recipes we were creating in a relatable, unpretentious way. And it resonated with other people. And so it began.

Brad

FAVORITE FOOD:
"There's so many—
cheese, burrata,
salami, prosciutto,
burritos. Oooh!
Prime rib!"

FAVORITE
ACTIVITIES:
Running and skiing

FAVORITE
HISTORICAL
FIGURE:
Ned Stark

FUN FACT:
Brad will eat
anything on this
planet . . . except
hard-boiled eggs.

Michelle

FAVORITE FOOD:
Olives (but really
string cheese)

FAVORITE SONG:
"Slow Dance," by
John Legend

FAVORITE ACTIVITY:
"Does getting a
massage count?"

FUN FACT:
Michelle won't
look in a mirror in
the dark.

Teagan

FAVORITE FOOD:
Sushi

FAVORITE SONG:
"Uptown Funk (ft.
Bruno Mars)," by
Mark Ronson

FAVORITE ACTIVITY:
Soccer

Camryn

FAVORITE FOOD:
Soft pretzel bites

FAVORITE MOVIE:
Descendants 3

FAVORITE ACTIVITY:
Horseback riding

26 KITCHEN HACKS, TIPS, AND TRICKS TO MAKE YOUR COOKING LIFE EASIER

My favorite number is 26, and it just never gets used for things. I mean, there is never a list of 26 of anything. So today I present to you 26 bits of cooking wisdom I've learned along the way that have made eating well and cooking more manageable.

1.

To pit cherries easily and without a mess, use a cherry pitter and pit the cherries inside a brown paper bag. The pitter pops the pit right out and the paper bag acts as a splash guard, preventing the cherry juice from staining your counter and pretty white shirt.

2.

Place frozen meat on a baking sheet for quick thawing. The metal pan conducts heat in a way that will expedite thawing and save you from all the times you forgot to #pulloutyourmeat. Thawing times will obviously vary depending on the amount of meat you've got, but expect times to be cut in half.

3.

Did you forget to throw a bottle of wine in the fridge prior to company arriving? Simply wrap a wet towel around the wine bottle and stick it in the freezer. Chill it for 30 to 40 minutes, and presto: cold wine! Run warm water over the frozen towel to release it from the bottle.

4.

Use a handheld mixer to shred chicken.

5.

Using a grease splatter screen while cooking on the stovetop will protect your stove from the otherwise inevitable layer of oily residue. It will cut down your stovetop cleaning and scrubbing time considerably.

6.

Broken eggshell in your bowl of cracked eggs? No problem! Simply use one of the eggshell halves to scoop out the broken bit. No need to get your fingers slimy while trying to grab that elusive little piece.

7.

Use a pair of clean pliers or tweezers to easily debone fish.

8.

When freezing fruit, wash the fruit, dry it, and place it on a flat surface, such as a rimmed baking sheet, then freeze it. Once the fruit is frozen solid, transfer it to a freezer-safe container. This prevents

the fruit from freezing into one big unmanageable clump.

9.

Nobody likes an unripe avocado. Nobody. To expedite ripening, place avocados in a paper bag with a ripe banana or two. (Bananas naturally release ethylene, which speeds up ripening.)

10.

If you drop an egg on the floor, simply pour ¼ cup of salt over it to make it quicker and easier to wipe up. The egg will absorb the salt, making for painless cleanup.

11.

Thinly slicing raw meat can be a bit difficult, since it is slippery and soft. Freeze meat for 20 minutes prior to cutting. The meat will harden just enough to make it easier to handle and slice properly, but will still be soft enough for a knife to cut through.

12.

When measuring a sticky ingredient like honey, lightly grease the measuring cup or spoon you're using prior to pouring in the ingredient. This ensures the entire amount of the sticky ingredient will slide right out—no scraping with a spatula required!

13.

A fried egg turns everything into a meal. Throw it over the top and call it a day.

14.

Tinkering in the kitchen without a recipe and unsure how much salt to add to meat or fish? You can't exactly taste the raw protein to find out, so what to do? I recommend using 1 teaspoon salt for every pound of protein you're working with, or 1¼ teaspoons, if you tend to like things on the saltier side.

15.

If you don't have a milk frother, pour your latte ingredients into a blender and pulse four or five times to create a foamy drink.

16.

Add sliced onions to a jar of leftover pickle or pepperoncini juice for a tangy topping to use on hamburgers. Simply add the onion slices to the brine, seal the jar, and let them marinate for 5 to 7 days before you want to use them. They'll keep for about two weeks if you store in an airtight jar.

17.

Save leftover Parmesan or Pecorino Romano rinds to add to soups

for extra flavor. Add them while the soup simmers and pull them out before serving.

18.

To break a head of cauliflower into florets without making a mess, leave the cauliflower in its wrapper and bang the stem end forcefully on the counter. My friend Jenn from the blog *Pretend It's a Donut* taught me this one, and it's a keeper!

19.

Store ginger in the freezer. Not only will it last longer, but it will be easier to grate on a Microplane.

20.

Use an ice cream scoop to form meatballs.

21.

Pulse brussels sprouts in a food processor or blender to shred them quickly.

22.

To keep parchment paper from sliding all over the baking sheet, crumple it up, then smooth it out prior to laying it on the pan.

23.

Use a potato masher to mash avocados for guacamole.

24.

To revive leftover rice, sprinkle it with some water prior to microwaving it.

25.

Get yourself an instant-read thermometer. It takes the guesswork out of cooking proteins and ensures your meat won't be overcooked.

26.

Invest in a sharp pair of kitchen shears. They make deboning chicken, cutting bacon, and snipping herbs so easy!

chapter 1

make ahead, keep on hand

WHILE I UNDERSTAND that we can't make every single condiment, spice, and dressing from scratch, it's handy to have a stock of homemade meal add-ons readily available for quick additions to proteins, vegetables, and salads through the week.

Taking just a few minutes out of your day to prep items such as these will save you loads of time and enable you to make healthy decisions when you're in a pinch.

14	Sweet Potato and Sage Zoodle Sauce
16	Chai Spice Blend
19	Honey-Curry Dip
20	Vegan Pesto
23	Creamy Romesco Sauce
24	Zesty Dill-Kefir Dressing
27	Chocolate Coco Whip
28	Cilantro-Jalapeño Aïoli
31	Strawberry-Feta Vinaigrette
32	Dairy-Free Cinnamon Maple Cashew Coffee Creamer
35	One-Minute Mayo

Sweet Potato and Sage Zoodle Sauce

MAKES
2 CUPS

Dairy-Free

Gluten-Free

Grain-Free

*Nut-Free
(option)*

Paleo

Vegan

Vegetarian

Full disclosure: I'm not a huge fan of marinara sauce. (I know, blasphemous.) I'm very *meh* about most of them. I think they tend to be a little too watery when paired with most spiralized vegetables. Veggie noodles are everywhere these days, and I feel they deserve a sauce that can stand up to them without getting watered down. Enter this sauce. While you *will* want to eat it by the spoonful, please save some for your dish. If you aren't on the veggie noodle train, this sauce is just as delicious over traditional pasta.

1 **pound sweet potatoes (usually 1 large will do)**

2 **teaspoons extra-virgin olive oil**

½ **onion, chopped**

3 **garlic cloves, minced**

3 **fresh sage leaves**

¾ **cup unsweetened plain almond milk (see Tip)**

¾ **teaspoon salt**

⅛ **teaspoon freshly ground black pepper**

tip: Use coconut milk in place of the almond milk, if someone has a tree nut allergy.

Preheat the oven to 450°F.

Use a fork to puncture holes in the sweet potatoes. Place on a baking sheet and bake until soft inside and easily pierced with a fork, about 45 minutes, depending on the size of the sweet potatoes. Remove from the oven and set aside to cool slightly.

While the sweet potatoes are baking, in a small saucepan over medium heat, heat 1 teaspoon of the olive oil. When the oil is hot, add the onion and cook, stirring occasionally, until the onion is soft, 6 to 7 minutes. Add the garlic and cook, stirring, until the onion is tender, 1 minute more. Transfer the onion and garlic to a blender or food processor.

Add the remaining 1 teaspoon oil to the saucepan. When the oil is hot, add the sage leaves. Cook until they are lightly fried, about 1 minute on each side, then transfer to the blender.

Scrape the flesh of the sweet potatoes into the blender; discard the skins. Add the almond milk, salt, and pepper. Blend on high until the sauce is smooth and creamy.

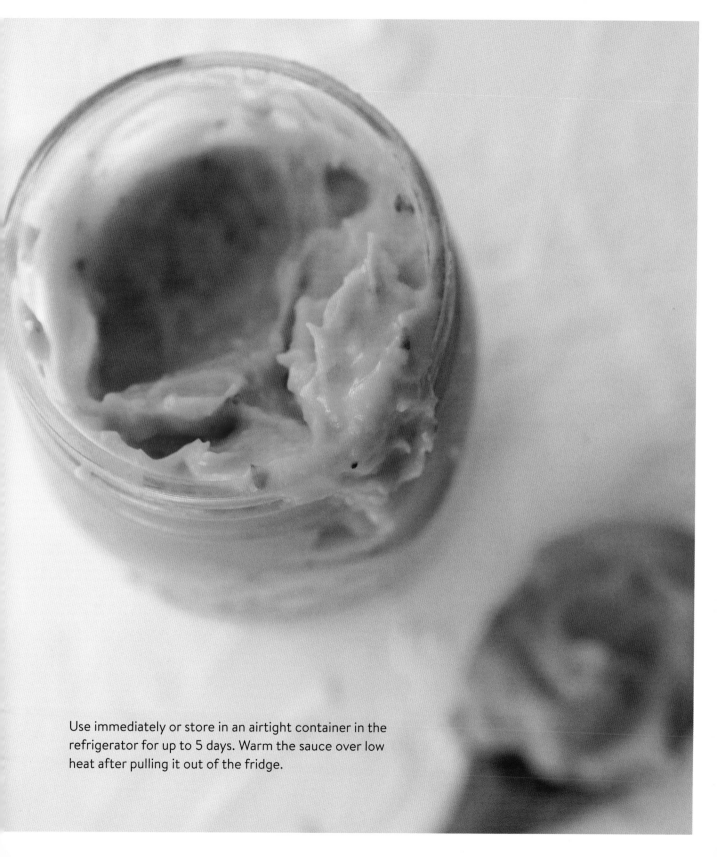

Use immediately or store in an airtight container in the refrigerator for up to 5 days. Warm the sauce over low heat after pulling it out of the fridge.

Chai Spice Blend

MAKES
ABOUT
¼ CUP

Dairy-Free

Gluten-Free

Grain-Free

Nut-Free

Paleo

Vegan

Vegetarian

Is it safe to say chai spice is the grown-up version of cinnamon? I love the layered levels of flavor that chai spice can bring to food. From lattes to roasted carrots to desserts, chai spice increases the yum factor tenfold, in my opinion. I don't find chai spice blends readily available at most grocery stores, so I decided to create one. If you find that you're regularly adding chai spice to your dishes, by all means, double this recipe.

1 tablespoon ground cinnamon

1 tablespoon ground ginger

2 teaspoons ground cardamom

1 teaspoon ground allspice

1 teaspoon ground cloves

1 teaspoon ground nutmeg

Pinch of freshly ground black pepper

Combine the cinnamon, ginger, cardamom, allspice, cloves, nutmeg, and pepper in a small airtight container. Store in a cool, dry place.

Honey-Curry Dip

MAKES
ABOUT 1 CUP

Dairy-Free

Gluten-Free

Grain-Free

Nut-Free

Paleo

Vegetarian

I'm pretty sure I could eat *anything* with this flavorful dip. Two of my favorite options are roasted sweet potato fries and rotisserie chicken, but any veggie or protein would be equally delicious.

1 cup One-Minute Mayo (page 35)

1 tablespoon honey

2 teaspoons curry powder

1 teaspoon coconut milk (full fat is preferred)

¼ teaspoon salt

¼ teaspoon freshly ground black pepper

Stir together the mayonnaise, honey, curry powder, coconut milk, salt, and pepper in an airtight container. Cover and store in the refrigerator for up to 5 days.

tip: Add an additional ¼ cup coconut milk to this dip to thin it out to use as a dressing.

Vegan Pesto

MAKES
ABOUT
2 CUPS

Dairy-Free

Gluten-Free

Grain-Free

Paleo

Vegan

Vegetarian

I used to think you couldn't make a delicious pesto without Parmesan. I mean, doesn't cheese make everything better? Well, as it turns out, it doesn't. You don't need cheese to make a delicious pesto. In lieu of cheese, I use some salted cashews—I find they mimic the taste of the traditional Parmesan perfectly: slightly nutty, sweet, and salty. Boom: vegan pesto. Try this in the Chicken and Pesto-Stuffed Sweet Potatoes on page 215 or the Pesto Shrimp and Cauli Puree on page 172.

4	cups loosely packed fresh basil leaves
4	garlic cloves
1	cup extra-virgin olive oil
½	cup salted roasted cashews
½	cup pine nuts, toasted (see Tip)
2	teaspoons salt

Combine the basil, garlic, olive oil, cashews, pine nuts, and salt in a blender or food processor. Blend on high speed for 10 to 15 seconds, until the nuts are broken down and the pesto is well combined but still has some texture.

Store in an airtight container in the refrigerator for up to 1 week. You can also freeze it in an ice cube tray for up to 6 months and pop out the frozen pesto cubes as needed.

tip: *To toast pine nuts, heat a small skillet over medium heat. When the pan is hot, add the pine nuts and toast, stirring them frequently, until they are golden brown, 1 to 2 minutes. Keep an eye on them, as they can burn quickly! Remove them from the pan as soon as they are done and let cool.*

Creamy Romesco Sauce

MAKES
ABOUT
2 CUPS

Dairy-Free

Gluten-Free

Grain-Free

Paleo

Vegetarian

Oh, man, is there anything this sauce doesn't pair well with? I love serving it alongside some roasted potatoes or over chicken or grilled fish. You can even serve it as a dip with some fresh veggies when you have company over.

1   (6-ounce) jar fire-roasted red peppers, drained

½   cup extra-virgin olive oil

2   garlic cloves

½   cup slivered almonds

1   tablespoon chopped, fresh flat-leaf parsley leaves

1   tablespoon red wine vinegar

1   teaspoon smoked paprika

½   teaspoon salt

    Pinch of red pepper flakes

2   tablespoons One-Minute Mayo (page 35)

Combine the roasted red peppers, olive oil, garlic, almonds, parsley, vinegar, paprika, salt, and red pepper flakes in a blender or food processor. Pulse until the sauce is a uniform consistency and relatively smooth. Transfer the mixture to a bowl and add the mayonnaise. Stir until the mayo is well incorporated.

Store in an airtight container in the refrigerator for up to 1 week.

Zesty Dill-Kefir Dressing

**MAKES
ABOUT
1½ CUPS**

Gluten-Free

Grain-Free

Nut-Free

Vegetarian

In case you're not familiar with kefir, it's a fermented milk drink. And you know what fermented means? Probiotics! Every time I see "fermented," I know I'm going to be getting a healthy dose of good bacteria for my gut. Think of kefir as liquid yogurt. It makes a great base for sauces and dressings, and this tasty, herby recipe is no exception. Make sure to use a full-fat kefir, as others will be too thin.

1½ **cups full-fat plain kefir**

1 **garlic clove**

1 **teaspoon salt**

½ **teaspoon lemon zest**

¼ **teaspoon freshly ground black pepper**

¼ **teaspoon onion powder**

2 **tablespoons finely chopped fresh dill**

Combine the kefir, garlic, salt, lemon zest, pepper, and onion powder in a blender and blend on high speed for 5 seconds, or until combined. Transfer to a jar and stir in the dill.

Cover and store in the refrigerator for up to 1 week.

note: *Adding the dill to the blender with the other ingredients may give the dressing a greenish hue. I prefer to chop the dill by hand and stir it in at the end.*

Chocolate Coco Whip

MAKES
ABOUT
2 CUPS

Dairy-Free

Gluten-Free

Grain-Free

Nut-Free

Paleo

Vegan

Vegetarian

Eat this whip with a spoon, dip strawberries into it, pour it over ice cream, or use it as a frosting. It doesn't matter what you do with it—it's delicious on everything.

1 **(13.5- to 14-ounce) can full-fat coconut milk, refrigerated for at least 8 hours**

2 **tablespoons pure maple syrup**

2 **teaspoons unsweetened cocoa powder**

Place the bowl of your stand mixer and the whisk attachment in the freezer for 30 minutes.

Open the can of coconut milk and scrape the hardened coconut cream from the top, leaving behind the liquid. Put the cream in the chilled stand mixer bowl and affix the bowl to your mixer. Whip the coconut cream on medium speed until it starts to get fluffy, 1 to 2 minutes. With the mixer running, slowly drizzle in the maple syrup. Add the cocoa powder and whip for 1 minute more, stopping and scraping down the sides of the bowl as needed, until the coconut cream is light and fluffy.

Store in an airtight container in the refrigerator for up to 1 week.

tips: *Not all coconut milks are created equal. I tested this recipe with several different brands and I found that coconut milk that contains no added ingredients—just coconut milk and water—works best and thickens the most. My personal favorite is the 365 Everyday Value brand from Whole Foods Market.*

I prefer to use a stand mixer for this recipe, but you can use a metal bowl and a handheld mixer instead. Just be sure to chill the bowl and beaters as directed.

Cilantro-Jalapeño Aïoli

MAKES
ABOUT 1 CUP

Dairy-Free

Gluten-Free

Grain-Free

*Nut-Free
(option)*

Paleo

Vegetarian

I think people fall into one of two categories: You're either a dipper or a non-dipper. I'm a dipper. I love dipping my food into a delicious sauce. I also love smothering my foods with delicious sauces. This dip is not only great for veggies, it also works as a topping on things like tacos and egg scrambles.

1 cup One-Minute Mayo (page 35)

½ medium jalapeño, seeds and ribs removed, chopped

1 garlic clove, chopped

1 tablespoon unsweetened plain almond milk (see Tips)

½ teaspoon lime zest

½ teaspoon salt

3 tablespoons chopped fresh cilantro

Combine the mayonnaise, jalapeño, garlic, almond milk, lime zest, and salt in a food processor and process for 6 to 7 seconds, until the ingredients are well mixed. Add the cilantro and pulse three or four times, until the cilantro is incorporated.

Store in an airtight container in the refrigerator for up to 5 days.

tips: To make this nut-free, use light coconut milk instead of almond milk.

Thin out this aïoli with an additional 1 tablespoon almond (or coconut) milk to transform it into a dressing.

Strawberry-Feta Vinaigrette

MAKES
ABOUT
¼ CUP

Gluten-Free

Grain-Free

Nut-Free

Vegetarian

While this zippy dressing can be served on all sorts of salads, I especially enjoy it over a spinach salad. You can even use it to top a piece of grilled salmon for an extra kick of flavor.

½ cup extra-virgin olive oil

1 tablespoon no-sugar-added strawberry jam

1 tablespoon champagne vinegar or white vinegar

¼ teaspoon salt

1 ounce feta cheese, crumbled (about ¼ cup)

Combine the olive oil, jam, vinegar, and salt in a blender and blend on high speed for 5 to 10 seconds, until the dressing has emulsified. Add the feta and pulse several times, until the feta is incorporated.

Store in an airtight container in the refrigerator for up to 5 days. Shake well before using.

xo

Dairy-Free Cinnamon Maple Cashew Coffee Creamer

MAKES
ABOUT
2 CUPS

Dairy-Free

Gluten-Free

Grain-Free

Paleo

Vegan

Vegetarian

I know, making your own coffee creamer sounds like it could be a nightmare, right? But with a bit of patience (let those cashews soak!) and a blender, it's a breeze. Try it in my Dairy-Free Cold-Brew Latte (page 106) for an extra-refreshing treat.

1	cup raw unsalted cashews
3¼	cups water
1	tablespoon pure maple syrup
1	teaspoon pure vanilla extract
⅛	teaspoon ground cinnamon
	Pinch of salt

Place the cashews in a bowl, add 2 cups water, and set aside at room temperature to soak for 10 to 24 hours.

Drain the cashews and put them in a blender or food processor. Add 1¼ cups water, the maple syrup, vanilla, cinnamon, and salt. Blend on high speed for about 1 minute, until the cashews are completely pureed and the mixture is smooth.

Store in an airtight container in the refrigerator for up to 1 week. Shake well before using.

tip: The longer the cashews soak, the creamier the creamer will be. So let them soak for a while, 'k?

One-Minute Mayo

MAKES
1 GENEROUS
CUP

Dairy-Free

Gluten-Free

Grain-Free

Nut-Free

Paleo

Vegetarian

I'm gonna be honest. This recipe was in my last cookbook. This recipe is on my website. And this recipe is in this cookbook. Can you guess why? Because it's *that* good! It's a game-changer. This olive oil–based mayo can be used as a creamy base for so many dressings, dips, and sauces, you're definitely going to want to keep it handy. As an added bonus, it's so fun to make!

1   cup extra-light-tasting olive oil (I like Bel'Olio)

1   large egg

1   teaspoon Dijon mustard

½   teaspoon fresh lemon juice

¼   teaspoon salt

In a tall, widemouthed mason jar or similar container, combine the olive oil, egg, mustard, lemon juice, and salt. Let the ingredients settle for a moment.

Place an immersion blender in the jar directly over the egg yolk and turn it on. Blend, without moving the blender, for 5 seconds to begin to emulsify the oil and egg, then very slowly move the blender up and down until the oil and egg are fully emulsified, about 30 seconds more.

Cover and store in the refrigerator for up to 1 week.

chapter 2

get set, meal prep!

WE ALL KNOW that preparing meals ahead of time makes eating healthy manageable. It's straight science. Personally, the times I make the worst food choices are the times I've waited too long to eat, haven't planned ahead, or have nothing on hand.

By keeping a few ready-made meals in your fridge or freezer, you'll save yourself the agony of having to pick up a frozen pizza on the way home from work. Because you know what? Frozen pizza sucks and is never worth it.

Taking the extra time to care for your future self is the ultimate self-care.

39	Banana Bread Overnight Oats
40	Breakfast Sausage Meatballs
43	Apple-Cinnamon Mini Frittatas
45	Arugula Melon Prosciutto Bowls
46	Orange-Ginger Smoothie Packs
49	Hearty Mediterranean Salad with Lemon-Dill Dressing
50	Sweet Potato Hash Egg Cups
53	Ground Beef Trifle with Cauliflower Puree
55	Hangry Man Plate
58	Buffalo Chicken Frittata

Banana Bread Overnight Oats

SERVES 4

Dairy-Free

Gluten-Free

Vegan (option)

Vegetarian (option)

Have you made overnight oats yet? They're, like, all the rage on the internet. And when the internet says to do something . . . you usually *shouldn't*. (Um, hello, #kyliejennerlipchallenge.)

However, when everyone is posting jars of easy-to-make overnight oats on their Pinterest boards, you should pay attention. You make these oats simply by soaking them overnight with lots of delicious add-ons. In this case, those add-ons give the oats the flavor of freshly baked banana bread.

The internet isn't always right . . . but in this case, it is.

2	ripe bananas
2½	cups gluten-free oats
3	cups unsweetened vanilla almond milk
½	cup raw walnut pieces
2	tablespoons collagen peptides (optional; see Tip)
2	tablespoons unsweetened shredded coconut
¼	cup pure maple syrup
4	teaspoons ground golden flaxseeds
4	teaspoons chia seeds
½	teaspoon ground cinnamon
¼	teaspoon salt
¼	cup fresh berries of your choice, for serving (optional)

Mash the bananas in a large bowl until they have the consistency of baby food. Add the oats, almond milk, walnuts, collagen peptides (if using), shredded coconut, maple syrup, flaxseeds, chia seeds, cinnamon, and salt. Stir to combine well.

Divide the oat mixture evenly among four mason jars or other airtight containers. Cover and refrigerate overnight.

To serve, stir the oats and top with fresh berries, if desired.

tip: *Omit the collagen peptides to make these oats vegetarian and vegan.*

Breakfast Sausage Meatballs

MAKES 24
MEATBALLS
(4 TO 6
SERVINGS)

Dairy-Free

Gluten-Free

Grain-Free

Nut-Free

Paleo

The only thing better than homemade breakfast sausage patties is homemade breakfast sausage *meatballs*. Somewhere along the line, we all decided that meatballs are more fun than flat patties, and that certainly holds true with this recipe. These are perfect to make ahead and have on hand to reheat for a quick and tasty breakfast when you have to run out the door.

2	pounds ground pork
4	fresh sage leaves, minced
1	tablespoon pure maple syrup
2½	teaspoons salt
1	teaspoon freshly ground black pepper
½	teaspoon cayenne pepper
½	teaspoon ground nutmeg
¼	teaspoon fennel seeds
⅛	teaspoon ground cloves

Preheat the oven to 400°F. Line a rimmed baking sheet with parchment paper and place a wire rack on top of the parchment.

Put the pork, sage, maple syrup, salt, black pepper, cayenne, nutmeg, fennel seeds, and cloves in a large bowl and use your hands to combine well. Roll the pork mixture into balls, using about 1½ tablespoons for each, and arrange them on the rack, spacing them evenly.

Bake the meatballs for 25 to 30 minutes, until they are lightly browned on the outside, cooked through, and no longer pink on the inside. Remove from the oven and let cool on the rack.

Store in a zip-top plastic bag in the refrigerator for up to 1 week or in the freezer for up to 3 months.

Apple-Cinnamon Mini Frittatas

MAKES 12 MINI FRITTATAS

Dairy-Free

Gluten-Free

Grain-Free

Nut-Free

Paleo

Vegetarian

I've become pretty good at predicting which of my recipes will become blockbusters, and this, my friends, is one of those recipes. Not only are these mini frittatas a breeze to make—they are downright addictive. You can serve them warm or cold. You can store them in the refrigerator for up to five days . . . if they make it that long. Personally, I prefer them cold, straight out of the fridge.

2 teaspoons coconut oil

1 Granny Smith apple, peeled, cored, and chopped into bite-size pieces

1½ teaspoons ground cinnamon
   Pinch of salt

9 large eggs

¼ cup honey

½ teaspoon pure vanilla extract

Preheat the oven to 375°F. Line a muffin tin with silicone muffin cups and grease the cups with 1 teaspoon of the coconut oil.

In a large skillet over medium heat, melt the remaining 1 teaspoon coconut oil. When the oil is hot, add the apple, ½ teaspoon of the cinnamon, and the salt. Cook, stirring occasionally, until the apple is tender, 5 to 6 minutes. Remove from the heat and let cool slightly.

Whisk together the eggs, honey, vanilla, and remaining 1 teaspoon cinnamon in a medium bowl until the honey dissolves and the mixture is well combined.

Divide the apple pieces among the prepared muffin cups. Pour in the egg mixture, filling the liners two-thirds of the way. Bake the mini frittatas for 13 to 15 minutes, until the eggs are cooked through and no longer runny.

Serve hot or at room temperature. Or let cool, then pop the frittatas out of the cups and store them in an airtight container in the refrigerator for up to 5 days. To reheat, simply microwave a frittata for 20 seconds.

tip: Make sure to lightly grease the silicone muffin cups to ensure that the frittatas pop out flawlessly every time.

Arugula Melon Prosciutto Bowls

SERVES 4

Dairy-Free (option)

Gluten-Free

Grain-Free

Nut-Free

Paleo

This bowl is the tastiest little bowl you could imagine, and it is almost too simple to believe. Whether you have it as an egg-free breakfast or a quick lunch, I promise you'll be satisfied. And probably want another helping.

8 cups baby arugula

2 teaspoons extra-virgin olive oil

Coarse salt

2 cups melon balls (honeydew and cantaloupe are great choices)

8 slices prosciutto

1⅓ cups plain whole-milk Greek yogurt or nondairy yogurt

4 teaspoons honey

Chile-lime seasoning, such as Tajín or Trader Joe's Chile Lime Seasoning Blend

Layer 2 cups of the baby arugula in the bottom of each of four bowls. Drizzle ½ teaspoon of the olive oil over the top and sprinkle with a pinch of the coarse salt.

Top each bowl with ½ cup of the melon, 2 slices of the prosciutto, and ⅓ cup of the yogurt. Drizzle 1 teaspoon of the honey over the top of the yogurt and season to taste with chile-lime seasoning. Serve immediately.

tips: To prevent the arugula from wilting, I recommend prepping and portioning the ingredients ahead and storing them separately. Take a minute or two to assemble a bowl just before you want to serve it. There's no reason to have wilted arugula, now, is there?

To make this recipe dairy free, simply use your favorite dairy-free yogurt.

Orange-Ginger Smoothie Packs

Dairy-Free

Gluten-Free

Grain-Free

Nut-Free

Paleo

*Vegan
(option)*

*Vegetarian
(option)*

Having ready-made smoothie packs stored in the freezer has been such a help on busy days and when my fridge is bare. They're a quick and easy way to get nutrients in when we otherwise may not be able to. And they're fun to make with clementines—we call them "baby oranges" in our home.

SMOOTHIE PACKS

10	clementine oranges, peeled and segmented
2½	ripe bananas, sliced
2½	cups fresh pineapple chunks
2½	cups grated carrots
5	(1-inch) pieces fresh ginger, peeled
3	tablespoons plus 1 teaspoon golden flaxseeds

FOR EACH SMOOTHIE

1¼	cups nondairy milk of your choice (I recommend almond, light coconut, or oat)
1	serving protein powder or collagen peptides of your choice (optional; see Tip)

To make the smoothie packs: Evenly divide the clementine segments, banana slices, pineapple, carrots, and ginger among five zip-top bags. Add 2 teaspoons flaxseeds to each bag. Press as much air out of the bags as you can, then seal them.

Store the smoothie packs in the freezer until you are ready to use them, up to 3 months.

To make one smoothie: Pour the contents of one smoothie pack into a blender and add the nondairy milk and protein powder or collagen peptides (if using). Blend on high speed until the smoothie is well blended. Serve immediately.

tip: *Use the serving size indicated by the manufacturer of the protein powder or collagen peptides. To make this recipe vegan or vegetarian, omit the collagen peptides and add your favorite vegan or vegetarian protein powder instead.*

Hearty Mediterranean Salad with Lemon-Dill Dressing

MAKES
5 SALADS
AND ABOUT
1 CUP
DRESSING

Gluten-Free

Grain-Free

Nut-Free

Vegetarian

This isn't just your run-of-the-mill Mediterranean salad, my friends. It's one that's designed to supercharge your day and leave you feeling satiated. When I go for a salad, I'm not looking for a salad that's loaded with lettuce—I want the *stuff*! And lettuce be real: Iceberg is just a cheap filler restaurants try to trick us with to make a quick buck. When did we start accepting salad as simply mediocre greens and dressing? Fill me *up*. And that's just what this recipe does: Fill. You. Up. With all the *stuff*.

LEMON-DILL DRESSING

- ¾ cup extra-virgin olive oil
- ¼ cup loosely packed fresh dill
- 3 garlic cloves, minced
- 3 tablespoons fresh lemon juice
- 2 teaspoons salt
- ⅛ teaspoon freshly ground black pepper

SALAD

- 5 cups baby arugula
- 1 medium cucumber, sliced
- 1 red bell pepper, diced
- 1¼ cups cherry tomatoes, halved
- 1¼ cups cooked lentils
- 1 (15-ounce) can chickpeas, drained and rinsed
- 1¼ cups kalamata olives, halved and pitted
- 5 tablespoons crumbled feta cheese

To make the dressing: Combine the olive oil, dill, garlic, lemon juice, salt, and pepper in a blender or food processor and pulse until the dressing is emulsified. Transfer to an airtight jar or five small airtight containers and cover.

Store in the refrigerator for up to 1 week.

To prepare the salad: Divide all of the prepped ingredients, minus the baby arugula, among five airtight containers. Store in the refrigerator.

When ready to serve, plate one cup of the baby arugula and top with one container of the remaining ingredients. Shake the dressing to re-emulsify it, if necessary, and drizzle the salad with the dressing to taste.

Sweet Potato Hash Egg Cups

MAKES
12 EGG CUPS

Dairy-Free
Gluten-Free
Grain-Free
Nut-Free
Paleo

I adore sweet potato hash for breakfast. I could eat it every day, truth be told. But it's kind of hard to eat in the car when you're in a rush on a busy morning. In fact, you should *not* attempt that. Ever. But you *can* grab a few of these Sweet Potato Hash Egg Cups and nosh on them, distraction- and mess-free. In the car, at school, at your desk. Anywhere. All the taste, none of the mess.

1   **teaspoon coconut oil**

½   **medium sweet potato, grated (¾ to 1 cup)**

1   **teaspoon extra-virgin olive oil**

½   **teaspoon salt**

4   **slices bacon**

6   **large eggs**

1   **teaspoon everything bagel seasoning**

tip: Lightly greasing the silicone muffin cups is key to making these egg cups easy to pop out.

Preheat the oven to 425°F. Line a muffin tin with silicone muffin cups and lightly grease the cups with the coconut oil.

Stir together the sweet potato, olive oil, and salt in a medium bowl. Divide the mixture evenly among the prepared muffin cups and press it up the sides to form a cup. Bake for 16 to 18 minutes, until the sweet potato is soft.

While the cups are baking, heat a skillet over medium heat. Put the bacon in the pan and cook until crisp, 7 to 8 minutes. Transfer the bacon to a paper towel–lined plate to drain and cool.

Transfer the bacon to a blender or food processor and pulse to create bacon "bits."

Beat the eggs in a medium bowl. Add the bacon bits and bagel seasoning and stir to combine.

Pour the egg mixture into the sweet potato cups, filling about two-thirds up. Reduce the oven temperature to 375°F. Bake the egg cups for 16 to 18 minutes, until they are cooked through and the eggs are no longer runny.

Let the egg cups cool and store in an airtight container in the refrigerator for up to 5 days. Reheat in the microwave to serve.

Ground Beef Trifle with Cauliflower Puree

Ground beef TRIFLE!? *Friends* fans may recognize this one as a nod to the traditional English trifle that Rachel made one Thanksgiving. While Rachel may have thought a layer of jam would pair delightfully with ground beef, I realize that is not the case. You can, however, create an *actual* layered ground beef dish that really does taste delicious. And no, there are no layers of ladyfingers or jam in this one. Layer this recipe in one-pint widemouthed mason jars for convenient weekday lunches. Simply reheat one in the microwave for a healthy option when you're short on time. This recipe will make one jar for every weekday.

SERVES 5

Gluten-Free

Grain-Free

Nut-Free

Paleo

BEEF FILLING

- 3 teaspoons extra-virgin olive oil
- 2 pounds ground beef (I prefer 85/15)
- 3½ teaspoons salt
- 1 large yellow onion, chopped
- 4 garlic cloves, minced
- 3 tablespoons Worcestershire sauce
- 2 tablespoons tomato paste
- 4 teaspoons Dijon mustard
- ¼ cup red wine of your choice

CAULIFLOWER PUREE

- 1 head cauliflower (about 2 pounds), broken into florets
- 2 tablespoons butter or ghee
- 1½ teaspoons salt
  Fresh parsley leaves, for garnish (optional)

To make the beef filling: In a Dutch oven or large saucepan over medium heat, heat 2 teaspoons of the olive oil. When the oil is hot, add the ground beef and 2½ teaspoons of the salt. Cook the beef, gently breaking it up with a wooden spoon as it cooks, until it is browned and cooked through, 8 to 9 minutes. Using a slotted spoon, transfer the ground beef to a plate and set aside. Drain the fat from the pot.

In the same pot, heat the remaining 1 teaspoon olive oil over medium heat. When the oil is hot, add the onion and the remaining 1 teaspoon salt and cook, stirring occasionally, until the onion is translucent and soft, 7 to 8 minutes. Add the garlic and cook, stirring, for 1 minute more.

Return the ground beef to the pot and add the Worcestershire, tomato paste, mustard, and wine. Stir to combine. Cook over medium-low heat, stirring

continues

xo

**Ground Beef Trifle with Cauliflower Puree,
continued**

occasionally, until all the flavors have blended, 5 to 6 minutes.

To make the cauliflower puree: Fill a large pot with about 2 inches of water and bring to a boil. Insert a steamer basket and place the cauliflower florets in the basket. Cover the pot and steam the cauliflower for 5 to 7 minutes, until fork-tender. Transfer the cauliflower to a blender or food processor. Add the butter and salt and blend on high speed for about 10 seconds, until the cauliflower is a smooth puree.

To assemble the trifles: Fill five 1-pint widemouthed mason jars about halfway with beef filling. Spread about ½ cup of the cauliflower puree over the top. Garnish with parsley, if desired. Seal the jars.

Store in the refrigerator for up to 1 week. To reheat, remove the lid and microwave for 2 minutes.

Hangry Man Plate

Hangry (HANG-gree) *adjective*: bad-tempered or irritable as a result of hunger.
   Now that we all know *hanger* is a real thing that we've all suffered from at some point in our lives, I have just the remedy: an easy-to-make-ahead recipe that's ready for you whenever you feel hangry. This recipe packs up and reheats beautifully. In fact, it's one of those dishes that tastes even better the day after.

SERVES 4

Gluten-Free
Grain-Free
Nut-Free

TURKEY BREAST

- 1½ to 2 pounds skin-on, bone-in turkey breast, thawed if frozen
- 2½ teaspoons salt
- ¼ teaspoon freshly ground black pepper
- 1 tablespoon butter or ghee
- 1 tablespoon extra-virgin olive oil

MASHED POTATOES

- 3 pounds russet potatoes, peeled and cubed
- 1 tablespoon salt
- 3 tablespoons butter or ghee
- ½ cup unflavored nondairy creamer

MUSHROOM GRAVY
(recipe follows on next page)

To make the turkey breast: Preheat the oven to 350°F.

Use a finger to loosen the skin from the turkey flesh. Season the turkey all over with the salt and pepper, making sure to season under the skin.

Heat a cast-iron skillet over medium-high heat. When the skillet is hot, add the butter or ghee. Add the turkey skin-side down and sear until the skin is golden brown, 5 to 6 minutes. Flip the turkey so it's skin-side up and place the skillet in the oven. Roast the turkey for 35 to 45 minutes, until the internal temperature at the thickest point reaches 165°F. (Use your instant-read thermometer to check.)

To make the mashed potatoes: While the turkey is roasting, bring a large pot of water to a boil. Add the potatoes and cook for 10 to 15 minutes, until they are fork-tender. Drain the potatoes and return them to the pot. Add the salt, butter, and nondairy creamer. Mash the potatoes until they are smooth.

When the turkey is finished, very carefully remove the skillet from the oven and place it on the stovetop. Transfer the turkey to a plate and cover with aluminum foil. Let rest for 10 to 12 minutes and then slice.

continues

Hangry Man Plate, <u>continued</u>

MUSHROOM GRAVY

1½ pounds cremini mushrooms, sliced

1 teaspoon salt

3 garlic cloves, minced

½ cup plus 2 tablespoons turkey broth or chicken broth

¼ cup unflavored nondairy creamer

To make the mushroom gravy: Set the heat under the skillet to medium-high. (Be very careful, as the pan will still be hot from the oven!) Add the mushrooms and salt to the skillet and cook, stirring occasionally, until the mushrooms are soft and cooked through, 6 to 7 minutes. Add the garlic and cook for 1 minute more. Carefully transfer the contents of the skillet to a blender and add the broth and nondairy creamer. Blend on high until smooth.

Divide the mashed potatoes among four airtight microwave-safe storage containers, place several slices of turkey on top, and pour one-quarter of the gravy over the turkey.

Cover and store in the refrigerator for up to 5 days. To reheat, microwave for 2 minutes.

Buffalo Chicken Frittata

SERVES
4 TO 6

Gluten-Free

Grain-Free

Nut-Free

Paleo

Would this even be a relevant cookbook for the twenty-first century if it *didn't* include some sort of "Buffalo" recipe? I think not.

4 tablespoons butter or ghee

1 pound frozen hash browns, thawed

1½ teaspoons salt

8 large eggs

¼ cup light coconut milk

1 cup grated medium-sharp cheddar cheese

2 cups shredded cooked chicken (white and/or dark meat; rotisserie chicken is okay)

⅓ cup Frank's RedHot sauce

¼ teaspoon Worcestershire sauce

½ cup cherry tomatoes, halved

2 green onions, light green and white parts only, sliced

Preheat the oven to 350°F.

Heat a large cast-iron skillet over medium heat. When the pan is hot, add 2 tablespoons of the butter and let it melt, tilting the pan to coat the bottom. Add the hash browns in an even layer and sprinkle with 1 teaspoon of the salt. Brown the hash browns, without stirring, for 4 minutes, then flip them and cook until browned and crisped on the second side, 4 minutes more.

Whisk together the eggs, remaining ½ teaspoon salt, and the coconut milk in a medium bowl. Pour the egg mixture evenly over the hash browns, then add the cheese and chicken. Using a spatula, slowly stir everything for about 30 seconds to create large curds of eggs.

Place the skillet in the oven and bake the frittata for 8 to 9 minutes, until the eggs are no longer runny. Remove from the oven and let cool for about 10 minutes before serving.

While the frittata is cooling, stir together the hot sauce, Worcestershire, and remaining 2 tablespoons butter in a small saucepan. Heat over medium-low heat, stirring, until the sauce is combined.

Divide the frittata into 6 wedges and place them in a microwavable airtight container. Put the tomatoes, green onions, and sauce in separate containers and store in the refrigerator. To serve, reheat the frittata in the microwave for 1½ minutes and top with additional components.

chapter 3

aww, sheet

SHEET PANS HAVE BEEN AROUND since the dawn of cooking. Or close to it. Growing up, we usually pulled one out only for take-and-bake pizzas, but that's neither here nor there. Today, sheet pans are having a revival.

Desserts, full-on breakfasts, and crackers are all getting the sheet pan treatment from home cooks these days. In this chapter, I gather some of my favorite recipes that utilize the magic and convenience of the sheet pan. It's your one-stop shop for tasty food and easy cleanup.

Note that for all the recipes in this chapter, I use a standard rimmed half sheet pan (18 by 13 inches).

63	Spaghetti Squash Pizza
64	Grain-Free Everything Bagel Crackers
67	Sriracha Salmon and Broccoli
69	Sheet Pan Eggplant Parmesan
73	Oven-Roasted Cauliflower Rice
74	Spatchcocked Chimichurri Chicken and Carrot Fries
77	Sausages with Mustard Parsnips and Onions
79	Sheet Pan "Fried" Chicken and BBQ Kale Chips
83	Sheet Pan Beef Jerky
84	Sheet Pan Harissa Chicken and Veggies

Spaghetti Squash Pizza

GREAT for LEFTOVERS

SERVES
6 TO 8

Gluten-Free
Grain-Free
Nut-Free

In my first cookbook, I created a pizza soup that Brad deemed "pedestrian" before he even tried it. But once he did try it, of course he loved it. When I told Brad I was going to make a spaghetti squash pizza this time, he had ready all the "pedestrian" jokes you could imagine. Ha. Isn't he a charm? Well, I would like to report that he went back for seconds on this before I even had a chance to sit down and take my first bite. My kids, who aren't fans of spaghetti squash, also gobbled it down and had seconds. I think it's safe to say that "pedestrian" pizza renditions are the perfect formula for getting families to happily eat their veggies.

2 **medium spaghetti squash (3 to 3½ pounds each)**

4 **teaspoons extra-virgin olive oil, plus more for the pan**

2 **teaspoons salt**

½ **teaspoon dried oregano**

¼ **teaspoon freshly ground black pepper**

1 **(15-ounce) can pizza sauce**

8 **ounces fresh mozzarella, grated (about 2 cups)**

4 **ounces sliced pepperoni**

1 **green bell pepper, sliced**

¼ **small onion, thinly sliced**

1 **cup sliced pitted black olives**

   Red pepper flakes

   Flaky sea salt

Preheat the oven to 425°F.

Quarter the spaghetti squash lengthwise and place them cut-side up on a baking sheet. Drizzle the flesh of the squash with the olive oil and sprinkle with 1 teaspoon of the salt, the oregano, and the black pepper. Roast the squash for about 35 minutes, until the flesh is fork-tender. Remove the squash from the oven and let cool slightly (keep the oven on). When the squash is cool enough to handle, use a fork to scrape the flesh from the skins. Discard the skins.

Lightly grease the baking sheet with olive oil and spread the spaghetti squash over the pan in an even layer. Sprinkle the remaining 1 teaspoon salt over the squash. Pour the pizza sauce over the squash and use a spoon to spread it evenly. Sprinkle the mozzarella evenly over the sauce and arrange the pepperoni over the cheese. Top with the bell pepper, onion, and olives. Return the pan to the oven and bake for 25 minutes, or until the cheese has melted.

Season each piece with red pepper flakes and flaky sea salt.

Grain-Free Everything Bagel Crackers

MAKES
24 TO 36
CRACKERS

Dairy-Free

Gluten-Free

Grain-Free

Paleo

Vegetarian

I know what you're thinking: "I ain't got no time to make crackers from scratch! Isn't this book supposed to be for every day?!" You gotta trust me. You'll be shocked by just how easy it is to make crackers at home. If it weren't, they wouldn't be in this cookbook. I kept the ingredient list to a minimum, and chances are you already have the ingredients in your pantry. They take just twenty minutes to bake up, with very little mess to clean up afterward. Whether you're making these for your kids to snack on or to serve to guests with a cheese plate, you can't go wrong.

2 large egg whites

1 large egg

¼ cup extra-virgin olive oil

1½ cups almond flour

¼ cup coconut flour

¼ cup tapioca flour

3 tablespoons everything bagel seasoning

1 teaspoon flaky sea salt

Preheat the oven to 375°F.

Whisk 1 egg white and the whole egg together in a bowl. Add the olive oil and 2 tablespoons water and whisk until well combined.

Stir together the almond, coconut, and tapioca flours and 2 tablespoons of the bagel seasoning in a medium bowl. Pour in the egg mixture and stir until the ingredients are well combined and form a crumbly dough. Work the dough into a ball using your hands.

Turn the dough out onto your work surface and separate it into two equal pieces. Place one portion of the dough between two pieces of parchment paper and roll it out to a ⅛-inch-thick rectangle, keeping the thickness as even as possible. Carefully remove the top piece of parchment and move the dough, still on the bottom layer of parchment, onto a baking sheet.

continues

Grain-Free Everything Bagel Crackers,
<u>continued</u>

Repeat with the second portion of the dough and place it on a second baking sheet.

Whisk the remaining egg white lightly and gently brush it over the rolled-out dough. Combine the flaky sea salt and the remaining 1 tablespoon bagel seasoning and sprinkle the mixture over the dough. Lightly press the seasonings into the dough.

Using a pizza cutter, cut the dough into 1½- to 2-inch squares. Bake the crackers for 20 to 22 minutes, until lightly browned. Transfer the crackers to a wire rack and let cool to room temperature. Once cool, break the crackers along the cuts.

Store in an airtight container at room temperature for up to 1 week.

Sriracha Salmon and Broccoli

**SERVES
4 TO 6**

Dairy-Free

Gluten-Free

Grain-Free

Nut-Free

Paleo

While I tend to monitor the levels of "spice" in my dishes so my kids can eat them, this dish is not one of those. The heat is what makes it! I mean, it's *sriracha*—it's supposed to have a kick to it.

But never fear—if you're worried about your kids not being down with the spice, you can modify the heat level for them. All you need to do is season their portion of salmon and broccoli with a bit of salt and bake it on its own pan. There's no need to make them a completely different meal. #justsaynotochickennuggets

½   cup coconut aminos

4   garlic cloves, minced

2   tablespoons sriracha

1   tablespoon toasted sesame oil

2   teaspoons seasoned
rice vinegar

2   teaspoons honey

1½   pounds skin-on salmon fillet,
cut into 4 to 6 pieces

2   teaspoons salt

1   pound broccoli florets (from
about 2 medium heads)

1   tablespoon extra-virgin
olive oil

tip: Try using leftover salmon in the Salmon and Pineapple Jicama Tacos on page 216.

Stir together the coconut aminos, garlic, sriracha, sesame oil, rice vinegar, and honey in a small bowl. Season the salmon fillets on both sides with 1 teaspoon of the salt and place them in a large bowl or zip-top plastic bag. Add the coconut amino mixture to the bowl and cover it with plastic wrap (or pour it into the bag and seal the bag) and marinate the salmon in the fridge for 1 hour.

Preheat the oven to 400°F.

Toss the broccoli with the olive oil and the remaining 1 teaspoon salt. Spread the broccoli over two-thirds of a baking sheet and bake for 12 minutes.

Remove the baking sheet from the oven. Remove the salmon from the marinade and place the salmon skin-side down on the exposed portion of the pan. Pour the marinade over the broccoli and salmon. Bake for 13 to 15 minutes, until the salmon is cooked through and flakes easily with a fork.

To serve, plate the broccoli alongside the salmon. Store leftovers in an airtight container in the refrigerator for up to 5 days.

Sheet Pan Eggplant Parmesan

SERVES 4 TO 6

Gluten-Free

Grain-Free (option)

Nut-Free

Vegetarian

When I first served this to my kids, I didn't tell them it was eggplant, knowing they would automatically protest. Instead I said it was a new pizza dish I was working on. They gobbled it up and couldn't stop eating it. They had seconds and even thirds. Needless to say, it was a hit. Toward the end of the meal, when I finally told them it was eggplant, they were shocked. If you're looking for a way to get some extra veggies in, this is a sneaky and safe way to do it.

1   globe eggplant (about 1 pound), sliced into ½-inch-thick discs

1½   teaspoons salt

1   cup almond flour

¼   cup plus 2 tablespoons tapioca flour

¼   cup crushed gluten-free crackers (see Tip)

½   teaspoon garlic powder

2   large eggs

2   cups marinara sauce

8   ounces fresh mozzarella, thinly sliced

½   cup grated Parmesan cheese

¼   cup chopped fresh basil

    Flaky sea salt

Place a baking sheet in the oven and preheat the oven to 425°F.

Sprinkle the eggplant slices with ½ teaspoon of the salt. Set them aside on paper towels to drain a bit.

Combine the remaining 1 teaspoon salt, the almond flour, tapioca flour, crushed crackers, and garlic powder in a shallow bowl. In a separate shallow bowl, lightly beat the eggs.

Dredge a slice of the eggplant in the egg and let the excess run off. Immediately dredge the eggplant in the flour-cracker coating to cover all sides. Set the breaded eggplant aside on a plate and repeat with the remaining eggplant slices.

Remove the hot pan from the oven (make sure to use oven mitts!) and lay the breaded eggplant slices on the pan in one layer. Bake for 30 minutes, flipping the eggplant slices halfway through, until they are lightly browned. Remove the pan from the oven and top each slice with a generous spoonful of the marinara

continues

Sheet Pan Eggplant Parmesan, continued

sauce, a slice of the mozzarella, and a sprinkle of the Parmesan. Bake the eggplant for 10 minutes more, until the cheeses have melted. Remove the pan from the oven.

Sprinkle the basil over the eggplant Parmesan, season with some flaky sea salt, and serve.

tip: To make this grain-free, use a grain-free cracker. My personal preference is one from Simple Mills.

Oven-Roasted Cauliflower Rice

SERVES
2 TO 4

Dairy-Free

Gluten-Free

Grain-Free

Nut-Free

Paleo

Vegan

Vegetarian

Soggy cauliflower rice is akin to walking around in soggy socks: mushy, squishy, and stinky.

However! *Roasted* cauliflower rice? It's magical. You'll get some lightly browned bits, a.k.a. flavor makers, and the texture will hold up perfectly against whatever it is you're pairing the cauliflower with.

To ensure that the cauliflower doesn't get overcrowded and cooks properly, you'll need two baking sheets for this recipe.

2 **pounds cauliflower, riced (about 4 cups)**

2 **tablespoons extra-virgin olive oil**

1 **teaspoon salt**

½ **teaspoon freshly ground black pepper**

Preheat the oven to 425°F. Line two baking sheets with parchment paper.

Combine the cauliflower, olive oil, salt, and pepper in a large bowl and stir to coat the cauliflower evenly. Divide the cauliflower rice between the parchment-lined baking sheets and spread it into a thin, even layer. Roast the cauliflower on the middle and top racks for 15 to 20 minutes, until the cauliflower starts to turn golden brown.

Serve, or let cool and store in an airtight container in the refrigerator for up to 4 days.

Spatchcocked Chimichurri Chicken and Carrot Fries

SERVES 4 TO 6

Dairy-Free

Gluten-Free

Grain-Free

Nut-Free

Paleo

Not only is "spatchcocked" fun to say, it's a great way to cook a chicken. You simply remove the backbone from the chicken and press down on the breastbone to splay the bird out, which makes for a shorter cooking time. *And* it increases the surface area of the chicken, ensuring you have the maximum amount of crispy chicken skin.

½ **cup plus 2 teaspoons extra-virgin olive oil**

10 **garlic cloves, minced**

½ **cup chopped fresh cilantro**

½ **cup chopped fresh flat-leaf parsley**

2 **teaspoons lime zest**

4 **teaspoons fresh lime juice**

1 **tablespoon plus 2½ teaspoons salt**

1 **teaspoon honey**

¼ **teaspoon red pepper flakes**

6 **medium carrots, cut into 4-inch-long, ½-inch-thick "fries"**

1 **(3- to 4-pound) whole chicken**

Preheat the oven to 425°F.

Combine ½ cup of the olive oil, the garlic, cilantro, parsley, lime zest, lime juice, 2 teaspoons of the salt, the honey, and the red pepper flakes in a medium bowl and stir to combine thoroughly. Pour half the chimichurri sauce into a separate bowl and set it aside.

Put the carrot "fries" in a large bowl, add 1 teaspoon of the olive oil and ½ teaspoon of the salt, and toss to coat. Lay the carrots on a baking sheet in an even layer.

Place the chicken on a cutting board, breast-side down, and locate the chicken's backbone. Using a sharp pair of kitchen shears, cut out the backbone. (Discard it or save it to make stock.) Flip the chicken over and press down on the breastbone to splay it out. Run your finger under the skin of the chicken, loosening the skin from the flesh. Stuff the chimichurri from one of the bowls under the skin of the chicken. Season the skin with the remaining

continues

**Spatchcocked Chimichurri Chicken
and Carrot Fries, <u>continued</u>**

1 tablespoon salt and brush with the remaining 1 teaspoon olive oil.

Place the chicken skin-side up directly on the carrots and roast for about 1 hour, until the skin is beginning to crisp and the internal temperature of the chicken reaches 165°F. (Use your instant-read thermometer to check.) Transfer the chicken to a cutting board and let it rest for 10 to 13 minutes.

Carve the chicken into serving pieces. Serve with the roasted carrot "fries" and the remaining chimichurri sauce alongside for dipping.

Sausages with Mustard Parsnips and Onions

SERVES
4 TO 6

Dairy-Free
Gluten-Free
Grain-Free
Nut-Free
Paleo

I have a love-hate relationship with sheet pan meals. I love the convenience and idea of dumping everything onto a baking sheet and being done, but the truth is, roasted food needs plenty of space to cook properly. The pretty photos of most sheet pan meals you see are usually arranged after the fact. When vegetables and meat are being roasted, they give off steam. If the food is arranged too closely on a pan, it will often steam rather than roasting. The simple fix is understanding that two pans usually work better than one. By using two baking sheets, you give the food proper room to roast and develop a rich flavor.

3 tablespoons extra-virgin olive oil

3 teaspoons Dijon mustard

2 teaspoons whole-grain mustard

2 teaspoons salt

1 teaspoon champagne vinegar or white wine vinegar

1¼ pounds parsnips, cut into 1- to 2-inch cubes

1 medium yellow onion, thinly sliced

6 chicken-apple sausages

1 cup sauerkraut, drained

Preheat the oven to 400°F. Line two baking sheets with parchment paper.

Whisk together the olive oil, Dijon mustard, whole-grain mustard, salt, and vinegar in a small bowl until emulsified.

Put the parsnips and onion in a large bowl and pour two-thirds of the mustard dressing over the top; reserve the remaining dressing for serving. Stir the vegetables to thoroughly coat.

Arrange the sausages on one prepared pan and the parsnips and onion in an even layer on the other. Bake everything for 35 to 40 minutes, until the parsnips and onion are tender and the sausages are lightly browned.

Serve with the remaining mustard dressing and the sauerkraut alongside.

AWW, SHEET

Sheet Pan "Fried" Chicken and BBQ Kale Chips

SERVES
4 TO 6

Dairy-Free
Gluten-Free
Grain-Free
Paleo

"Fried" chicken you can make on a sheet pan? That's grain-free? With a side of BBQ-flavored kale chips? Sign me up.

1½ **pounds chicken tenderloins**

4½ **teaspoons salt**

1 **teaspoon coconut sugar**

1½ **teaspoons smoked paprika**

1¼ **teaspoons garlic powder**

⅛ **teaspoon cayenne pepper**

1 **tablespoon extra-virgin olive oil**

½ **pound lacinato kale (about 10 leaves)**

1¼ **cups almond flour**

½ **cup tapioca flour**

2 **large eggs**

½ **cup barbecue sauce, for serving**

Position a rack in the center of the oven, place a baking sheet on the rack, and preheat the oven to 425°F. Line a second baking sheet with parchment paper.

Season the chicken with 2 teaspoons of the salt and set aside.

Stir together the coconut sugar, 1 teaspoon of the salt, ½ teaspoon of the paprika, ¼ teaspoon of the garlic powder, and the cayenne in a small bowl to make the barbecue seasoning. Massage the olive oil evenly into the kale leaves and season them with the barbecue seasoning. Lay them flat in one layer on the parchment-lined baking sheet and set aside.

Combine the almond flour, ¼ cup of the tapioca flour, the remaining 1½ teaspoons salt, remaining 1 teaspoon paprika, and remaining 1 teaspoon garlic powder in a large bowl and stir well. Put the remaining ¼ cup tapioca flour in a shallow bowl. Lightly beat the eggs in a separate shallow bowl.

Remove the hot pan from the oven (make sure to use oven mitts!).

Dredge a chicken tenderloin in the tapioca flour to coat, then dip it in the egg and let the excess drip off.

continues

AWW, SHEET

79

**Sheet Pan "Fried" Chicken and
BBQ Kale Chips, <u>continued</u>**

Dredge the tenderloin in the almond flour mixture to coat it completely. Lay it flat on the hot baking sheet and repeat with the remaining chicken tenderloins.

Bake the chicken tenderloins on the center rack for 15 minutes, or until they start to brown. Carefully flip the tenderloins with a metal spatula and return the pan to the center rack. At this point, put the baking sheet of kale in the oven on the top rack and bake the kale and chicken tenderloins together for 10 minutes, or until the kale is crispy and the tenderloins are golden brown all over.

Serve with the barbecue sauce alongside.

Sheet Pan Beef Jerky

SERVES
4 TO 6

Dairy-Free
Gluten-Free
Grain-Free
Nut-Free
Paleo

I remember longing for a fancy food dehydrator when I was a little girl. I'd watch the infomercial over and over again, wishing we had that magical machine. I couldn't understand why my mom always said no. Fast-forward to having my own kitchen and limited storage space, and I now understand why! The last thing I need is *another* appliance taking up precious kitchen real estate. The good news is, you don't need a giant dehydrator to make your own beef jerky at home, just a little patience.

1½	**pounds flank steak**
2½	**teaspoons salt**
½	**cup coconut aminos**
1	**tablespoon coconut sugar**
1	**teaspoon smoked paprika**
½	**teaspoon garlic powder**
½	**teaspoon freshly ground black pepper**

Cut the flank steak across the grain into ¼-inch-thick strips. Season the steak with the salt.

Combine the coconut aminos, coconut sugar, paprika, garlic powder, and pepper in a gallon-size zip-top bag. Seal the bag and shake gently to combine everything. Add the steak to the marinade and lightly agitate the bag to make sure it is well coated. Marinate the steak in the refrigerator for 12 to 24 hours.

Preheat the oven to 225°F. Line two sheet pans with wire racks.

Drain the steak and discard the marinade. Lay the strips of steak on the racks in one even layer. Bake for 2½ hours, or until the beef has dried out and is cooked through.

Store the jerky in an airtight container in the refrigerator for up to 1 week.

tip: *Place the flank steak in the freezer for 20 minutes prior to cutting it; this will make it much easier to thinly slice.*

Sheet Pan Harissa Chicken and Veggies

Harissa is a North African chile paste. Its main ingredient is roasted hot red peppers, combined with a lot of aromatic regional spices. Harissa tastes equally great on proteins as it does on vegetables.

SERVES 4

Dairy-Free (option)

Gluten-Free

Grain-Free

Nut-Free

Paleo

1	pound cauliflower florets (about ½ head)
¼	cup plus 1 teaspoon harissa
1	tablespoon plus 1 teaspoon extra-virgin olive oil
2½	teaspoons salt
1	teaspoon smoked paprika
2	medium zucchini, sliced crosswise ¼ inch thick
1½	pounds chicken tenderloins
½	cup canned chickpeas, drained and rinsed
½	cup pitted kalamata olives
1	ounce soft goat cheese, crumbled, for serving (optional; see Tip)

tip: To make this dairy-free, simply leave out the goat cheese.

Preheat the oven to 425°F.

Combine the cauliflower, ½ teaspoon of the harissa, 1 tablespoon of the olive oil, ½ teaspoon of the salt, and ½ teaspoon of the paprika in a large bowl and toss to coat. Arrange the cauliflower over one half of a baking sheet (set the bowl aside for the zucchini—no need to rinse it) and roast for 15 minutes.

While the cauliflower is roasting, in the same bowl, combine the zucchini, ½ teaspoon of the harissa, 1 teaspoon of the olive oil, ½ teaspoon of the salt, and the remaining ½ teaspoon paprika and toss to coat.

In a separate bowl, combine the chicken tenderloins, the remaining 1½ teaspoons salt, and the remaining ¼ cup harissa. Toss to coat the chicken well.

Remove the pan from the oven and arrange the zucchini in an even layer next to the cauliflower. Lay the chicken on the pan alongside the zucchini and bake for 15 to 17 minutes, until the chicken is almost cooked through and the vegetables are tender.

Scatter the chickpeas, goat cheese (optional), and olives over the chicken and vegetables and bake for 5 minutes more, or until the chicken is cooked through and no longer pink inside and the vegetables are soft.

chapter 4

five ingredients or less

NOTHING TURNS ME OFF from a recipe more than seeing that it has twenty-five ingredients, eighteen of which I don't have. While more complex ingredient lists have their place in some of my favorite recipes, busy weeknights are not usually the time for them.

I like keeping things simple for me to manage during the week, and that means fewer ingredients to prep, cook, and shop for. So five ingredients (or less) it is!

Before you say, "Hey! This recipe has seven ingredients," let's talk. We're not counting things like butter, milk, oil, salt, and pepper. Those are pantry staples, and you should have them on hand in your kitchen at any given time. In this chapter, when I say five or less, I'm talking about the main ingredients you might need to add to your grocery list and grab at the store. (If I *did* count things like olive oil and salt, do you know what you could make with five ingredients? Not much. A roasted carrot.)

With that said, enjoy these simple-to-make, easy-to-shop-for recipes. May they make your Wednesday nights all the more enjoyable.

89	Balsamic Chicken Thighs with Mushrooms and Caramelized Onions
91	Chipotle Smashed Potatoes
92	Plantain "French Toast" Dippers
95	Shrimp and Shishitos
96	Grilled Flank Steak with Tomato-Corn Salad
98	Pork and Maple Butternut Squash
101	Matcha-Kale Smoothie
103	Apple "Pasta"
104	Strawberry-Balsamic Beef Medallions
106	Dairy-Free Cold-Brew Latte
109	Firecracker Cauliflower
110	Pan-Seared Chicken and Crispy Shaved Brussels Sprouts
113	Chile-Lime Plantains
114	Caramelized Cherries and Yogurt

Balsamic Chicken Thighs with Mushrooms and Caramelized Onions

SERVES 4 TO 6

Dairy-Free (option)

Gluten-Free

Grain-Free

Nut-Free

Paleo

Sometimes it's unbelievable just how much flavor you can pack into a dish with just a few ingredients. It all comes down to how you maximize what each ingredient has to offer. In this recipe, I do that in a few different ways: First, I use the same pan for all the ingredients—cooking the chicken thighs first means all the rich chicken flavor in the drippings gets transferred to the onions and mushrooms. Second, I cook the onions slowly for an extended period of time. The longer the onions cook, the richer and more caramel-y they will be. Finally, I reduce the balsamic vinegar, giving it a sweeter depth that, in turn, enhances the other components. You don't need a lot of ingredients to create flavor, just the proper techniques to bring out the best of each ingredient.

2	**pounds boneless, skinless chicken thighs**
3½	**teaspoons salt**
¼	**teaspoon freshly ground black pepper**
½	**cup balsamic vinegar**
4	**tablespoons butter or ghee (see Tip)**
1½	**sweet onions, sliced about ½ inch thick**
1	**pound cremini mushrooms, sliced**
1	**tablespoon chopped fresh flat-leaf parsley, for garnish (optional)**

Season the chicken thighs with 2 teaspoons of the salt and the pepper and set them aside.

Pour the vinegar into a 6-inch-diameter saucepan and bring it to a simmer. Simmer over low heat for about 20 minutes, until the vinegar reduces to a light syrupy texture. Remove from the heat but keep warm.

While the vinegar is reducing, in a large skillet over medium heat, melt 2 tablespoons of the butter. When the butter is hot, add the chicken thighs. Cook until the thighs are cooked through and browned, 4 to 5 minutes on each side. Transfer the chicken to a plate, tent with aluminum foil, and let rest.

continues

Balsamic Chicken Thighs with Mushrooms and Caramelized Onions, <u>continued</u>

Add the onions and ½ teaspoon of the salt to the same pan. Cook the onions over medium heat, stirring occasionally, until they are tender and golden brown, 10 to 12 minutes. Remove the onions from the pan and set them aside in a bowl; cover loosely with foil.

Melt the remaining 2 tablespoons butter in the pan, still over medium heat. When the butter is hot, add the mushrooms and the remaining 1 teaspoon salt. Cook, stirring frequently, until the mushrooms are tender, about 10 minutes.

Return the chicken and onions to the pan and stir to combine them with the mushrooms, cooking just long enough to reheat the chicken and onions, 3 to 4 minutes.

To serve, plate the chicken, mushrooms, and onions and drizzle some of the balsamic reduction over the top. Garnish with the parsley, if desired.

tip: To make this dairy-free, substitute extra-virgin olive oil for the butter or ghee.

Chipotle Smashed Potatoes

Potatoes, chorizo, and chipotles? They make the perfect thruple, as evidenced by the flavors of this recipe. Use any leftovers in the Chipotle Potato Pancake Stacks on page 211.

**SERVES
6 TO 8**

Gluten-Free
Grain-Free
Nut-Free

4   **medium russet potatoes, peeled and cubed**

2   **teaspoons extra-virgin olive oil or avocado oil**

1   **medium onion, chopped**

1   **tablespoon plus ½ teaspoon salt**

1   **pound fresh (Mexican) chorizo, casings removed**

1   **cup unsweetened plain almond milk**

6   **tablespoons butter or ghee**

2   **canned chipotle chiles in adobo sauce, chopped, plus 2 teaspoons adobo sauce from the can**

Bring a large pot of water to a boil. Add the potatoes and boil until tender, 15 to 20 minutes. Drain the potatoes, return them to the pot, and set aside.

While the potatoes are boiling, in a medium skillet over medium heat, heat 1 teaspoon of the olive oil. When the oil is hot, add the onion and ½ teaspoon of the salt. Cook, stirring, until the onion is soft and lightly browned, 8 to 10 minutes. Remove the onion from the pan and set aside.

In the same pan, combine the remaining 1 teaspoon olive oil and the chorizo. Cook over medium heat, using a spatula to break apart the chorizo as it cooks, until lightly browned, 8 to 10 minutes. Drain off the excess fat.

Add the almond milk, butter, and remaining 1 tablespoon salt to the potatoes. Smash the potatoes until broken down—they don't need to be perfectly smooth.

Add the cooked onion, chorizo, chipotles, and adobo sauce to the potatoes. Stir to combine.

Serve. Store any leftovers in an airtight container in the refrigerator for up to 5 days.

Plantain "French Toast" Dippers

SERVES 4

Dairy-Free

Gluten-Free

Grain-Free

Nut-Free

Paleo

Vegan

Vegetarian

No, these little plantains aren't dipped in egg. And there's no bread. But they taste *just like French toast*! While I developed this recipe with tiny hands in mind, grown-ups will love them just as much.

⅓ cup coconut sugar

1 teaspoon ground cinnamon

⅛ teaspoon salt

½ cup coconut oil

4 slightly ripe (yellow) plantains, peeled and sliced into ¾-inch-thick discs

Pure maple syrup, for dipping

Cover a sturdy cutting board with several layers of paper towels.

Mix the coconut sugar, cinnamon, and salt in a shallow bowl. Set it aside.

In a large skillet over medium heat, melt the coconut oil. When the oil is hot, working in batches, add the plantains and cook them for 2 minutes on each side to soften them slightly. Using a slotted spoon, transfer them to the lined cutting board to drain.

When all the plantain slices have been cooked, smash them with the textured side of a meat tenderizer. (This will give them a waffle-like appearance.) Again, working in batches, return the smashed plantains to the hot oil and fry until they are lightly browned and crisp on the edges, about 1 minute on each side. Using the slotted spoon, remove them from the oil and immediately dredge them in the cinnamon-sugar. Set them on a wire rack while you fry the remaining plantain slices.

Serve with a small bowl of maple syrup alongside for dipping.

Shrimp and Shishitos

SERVES 4

Dairy-Free
Gluten-Free
Grain-Free
Nut-Free
Paleo

This dish is great served up on a platter as an appetizer for guests to nosh on. Or, if you're like Brad and me, as an afternoon snack for yourself.

4 tablespoons sweet chili sauce

¼ cup One-Minute Mayo (page 35)

1½ teaspoons toasted sesame oil

½ teaspoon extra-virgin olive oil

½ pound shishito peppers

¾ teaspoon salt

½ pound raw medium shrimp, peeled and deveined

2 garlic cloves, minced

Flaky sea salt

Mix 2 tablespoons of the sweet chili sauce and the mayonnaise in a small bowl and set it aside.

Heat a cast-iron skillet over medium-high heat. When the pan is hot, add 1 teaspoon of the sesame oil and the olive oil. When the oil is hot, add the shishitos and let sit, untouched, to blister the skins, 2 to 3 minutes. Once the skins start to blister, flip the shishitos and char the other side for 2 minutes. Remove the shishitos from the pan.

Add the remaining ½ teaspoon sesame oil to the pan. When the oil is hot, add the shrimp and cook them for 2 to 3 minutes on each side, until they are cooked through and pink. Add the garlic and cook for 1 minute more. Add the remaining 2 tablespoons sweet chili sauce to the pan and toss to coat the shrimp.

Plate the shishitos and shrimp on a large platter and season with flaky sea salt. Serve the bowl of dip on the side.

Grilled Flank Steak with Tomato-Corn Salad

SERVES 4 TO 6

Dairy-Free

Gluten-Free

Nut-Free

A good steak doesn't need much to be delicious. Proper seasoning and a light marinade are all it takes. Pair it up with some fresh summer veggies and call it a day. Use any leftover steak in the Sweet Potato Nachos on page 204.

2	pounds flank steak
1	tablespoon plus 2 teaspoons salt
¼	teaspoon freshly ground black pepper
½	cup coconut aminos
4	ears corn, husked
1	tablespoon extra-virgin olive oil
2	cups cherry tomatoes, halved
½	cup chopped fresh basil
4	teaspoons champagne vinegar

Season the flank steak on both sides with 1 tablespoon of the salt and the pepper. Place the steak and coconut aminos in a zip-top plastic bag and marinate in the refrigerator for 4 to 6 hours.

Prepare a grill for direct-heat cooking and heat it to medium-high.

Lightly coat the corn with the olive oil and place the ears on the grill over direct heat. Grill the corn, covered, for 15 to 20 minutes, rotating the ears halfway through, until the corn is easily pierced with a fork. Remove from the grill and let the ears cool until you can handle them. Cut the corn kernels off the cobs and put them in a bowl. (You should have about 2 cups of corn kernels.)

Place the steak on the grill and cook over direct heat until browned on the outside and lightly pink in the middle, about 5 minutes on each side for medium doneness. Transfer it to a platter, cover loosely with aluminum foil, and let rest for 10 minutes.

Add the tomatoes, basil, vinegar, and remaining 2 teaspoons salt to the bowl with the corn and stir to combine.

Thinly slice the steak across the grain. Plate the tomato-corn salad and serve the steak over the top.

Pork and Maple Butternut Squash

SERVES 6

Dairy-Free (option)

Gluten-Free

Grain-Free

Nut-Free

Paleo

Pork, maple, and butternut squash go together like Brenda, Brandon, and Dylan. Like championships, the Warriors, and Steph Curry. Like basil, tomato, and mozzarella. You get the idea—the flavors jam together perfectly.

1½ **pounds butternut squash, peeled, seeded, and cut into 1-inch cubes**

1 **tablespoon plus 1 teaspoon extra-virgin olive oil**

2 **teaspoons salt**

1½ **pounds boneless pork loin chops, 1½ to 2 inches thick**

2 **tablespoons butter (see Tip)**

1 **tablespoon pure maple syrup**

3 **fresh sage leaves, finely chopped**

Preheat the oven to 425°F. Line a baking sheet with parchment paper.

Toss the butternut squash, 1 teaspoon of the olive oil, and 1 teaspoon of the salt in a large bowl. Spread it on the parchment-lined baking sheet in an even layer. Roast for 30 to 40 minutes, until the squash is tender and lightly browned.

Meanwhile, season the pork chops with the remaining 1 teaspoon salt. Heat a cast-iron skillet over medium heat. Melt the butter and the remaining 1 tablespoon olive oil. When the oil is hot, add the pork chops and sear them for 3 to 4 minutes on each side to create a golden crust.

Place the skillet with the pork chops in the oven and roast for 15 minutes, or until the internal temperature of the pork reaches 145°F. (Use your instant-read thermometer to check.) Remove the skillet from the oven and transfer the pork chops to a plate. Cover them loosely with aluminum foil and let rest for 10 minutes.

continues

Pork and Maple Butternut Squash,
<u>continued</u>

If the squash is ready, remove it from the oven. If it needs more time, return the empty skillet to the oven to keep the pork drippings hot.

When the squash is done roasting, scrape it into the skillet with the pork drippings and add the maple syrup and sage. Stir well to coat the squash.

To serve, slice the pork chops and serve them over the squash. Pour any drippings from the pan over the top for additional flavor.

tip: *To make this dairy-free, substitute an additional 2 tablespoons olive oil for the butter.*

Matcha-Kale Smoothie

MAKES
1 SMOOTHIE

Dairy-Free

Gluten-Free

Grain-Free

Nut-Free

Paleo

*Vegan
(option)*

*Vegetarian
(option)*

I love a simple smoothie in the morning. But I need that smoothie to be packed with nutrients. The kale and matcha in this one are the ultimate nutrient power couple, loading it with vitamins and antioxidants.

1 cup light coconut milk or coconut milk beverage

½ cup crushed ice

1 frozen banana, cut into chunks

3 large lacinato kale leaves, torn into pieces

1½ teaspoons matcha powder

1 tablespoon collagen peptides (optional; see Tip)

Combine the coconut milk, ice, banana, kale, matcha powder, and collagen peptides (if using) in a blender. Blend on high speed for 30 seconds to 1 minute, until the smoothie is well blended. Serve immediately.

tip: To make this smoothie vegan and vegetarian, omit the collagen peptides.

Apple "Pasta"

Dairy-Free

Gluten-Free

Grain-Free

Paleo

Vegan

Vegetarian

Sure, you can just grab an apple and eat it, but where's the fun in that? Grab your spiralizer and have at it! Whether you eat this alone or on top of some vanilla ice cream is up to you. But it would be a shame to never know just *how* delicious this is with a bit of creamy vanilla ice cream, wouldn't you say?

4   **Granny Smith apples, peeled**

2   **tablespoons pure maple syrup**

1   **teaspoon ground cinnamon**

1   **teaspoon fresh lemon juice**

¼   **teaspoon pure vanilla extract**
    Pinch of salt

1   **tablespoon coconut oil**

Using the blade of your spiralizer that resembles a wide spaghetti noodle, spiralize the apples into a large bowl. Add the maple syrup, cinnamon, lemon juice, vanilla, and salt and toss to coat the apples well.

In a large skillet over medium heat, melt the coconut oil. When the oil is hot, add the apples. Cook, stirring occasionally, until the apples are tender, for 4 to 5 minutes.

Serve the apples warm, as is or over your favorite creamy treat.

Strawberry-Balsamic Beef Medallions

SERVES
4 TO 6

Gluten-Free

Grain-Free

Nut-Free

Whether you serve up these decadent bites on a platter as an appetizer at your next party or family style as a main dish on a Tuesday night is completely up to you. Either way, your family or friends will be delighted!

2 pounds filet mignon, cut into 1½-inch-thick medallions

4 teaspoons salt

½ teaspoon freshly ground black pepper

2 cups strawberries, hulled and quartered

½ cup balsamic vinegar

1 tablespoon extra-virgin olive oil

2 sweet onions, sliced

2 tablespoons butter

1 cup crumbled blue cheese (about 4 ounces)

Preheat the oven to 400°F.

Season the steaks with 2½ teaspoons of the salt and the pepper and let rest for 15 minutes.

Combine the strawberries and vinegar in a saucepan and cook over medium heat, stirring frequently with a spoon to gently break up the strawberries, for 6 to 7 minutes. Reduce the heat to maintain a simmer and cook until the mixture is a thick reduction, 7 to 8 minutes more. Set aside to keep warm.

In a medium skillet over medium heat, heat the olive oil. When the oil is hot, add the onions and remaining 1½ teaspoons salt. Cook, stirring frequently, until the onions are tender and lightly browned, 8 to 9 minutes. Set aside to keep warm.

In a cast-iron skillet over medium-high heat, melt the butter. When the butter is hot, add the steaks and sear for 2 to 3 minutes on each side. Transfer the skillet to the oven and bake until the internal temperature of the steaks reaches 145°F for medium doneness, or more or less time for your preferred doneness. (Use your instant-read thermometer to check.) Remove the skillet from the oven, transfer the steaks to a plate, and let them rest for 15 minutes.

To serve, cut the steaks into ½-inch-thick slices. Arrange the slices on a platter and top them with the strawberry-balsamic reduction, onions, and blue cheese.

Dairy-Free Cold-Brew Latte

MAKES
1 LATTE

Dairy-Free
Gluten-Free
Grain-Free
Paleo
Vegan
Vegetarian

Okay, so coffee aficionados may cringe—this isn't technically a "latte," since there's no milk and no espresso in it. But it's close enough, and just as tasty a treat on a warm day! It's a breeze to make and won't load you down with a ton of sugar like the lattes you can buy at your nearest chain coffee shop. I add some maca to it for additional nutrients. (Maca is a Peruvian plant that has been used to increase energy and stamina. If you don't have any maca on hand, no worries. It's just as delicious without it.)

½   cup cold-brew coffee

½   cup crushed ice

¼   cup nondairy creamer, homemade (see page 32) or store-bought

2   teaspoons pure maple syrup

¼   teaspoon maca powder

Combine the coffee, crushed ice, nondairy creamer, maple syrup, and maca powder in a mason jar, secure the lid, and shake for 10 to 15 seconds. Pour the latte into a glass, or enjoy straight from the jar.

Firecracker Cauliflower

SERVES 4

Dairy-Free
Gluten-Free
Grain-Free
Paleo
Vegan
Vegetarian

I called this recipe Firecracker Cauliflower not because it's so damn spicy and explosive (it's not *that* high on the spicy factor) but because someone should be launching a gorgeous fireworks display every time you take a bite. It is *that* good! Every. Single. Bite. Should be celebrated.

1   **head cauliflower, cut into bite-size florets**

1   **tablespoon plus 2 teaspoons avocado oil**

1   **teaspoon salt**

2   **tablespoons chili-garlic sauce**

2   **tablespoons coconut aminos**

1   **teaspoon fresh lime juice**

¼   **cup roasted salted peanuts, crushed**

Preheat the oven to 425°F. Line a baking sheet with parchment paper.

Toss the cauliflower, 1 tablespoon of the avocado oil, and the salt in a large bowl. Spread the cauliflower evenly on the parchment-lined baking sheet. Bake for 30 to 35 minutes, until the cauliflower is tender and lightly browned. (If you have some charred bits, even better! Char = flavor.)

Combine the remaining 2 teaspoons avocado oil, the chili-garlic sauce, coconut aminos, and lime juice in a small bowl. Add the crushed peanuts and stir.

When the cauliflower is done, transfer it to a clean large bowl and pour the sauce over the top. Gently stir the cauliflower to coat it with the sauce. Serve.

Pan-Roasted Chicken and Crispy Shaved Brussels Sprouts

SERVES 4

Dairy-Free

Gluten-Free

Grain-Free

Nut-Free

Paleo

It should be a cooking law that any time you roast chicken, you *must* cook some vegetables in the drippings in the pan. The added flavor is out of this world.

1	**pound boneless, skinless chicken breasts**
2	**teaspoons salt**
¼	**teaspoon freshly ground black pepper**
2	**teaspoons extra-virgin olive oil**
1	**tablespoon butter or ghee**
1½	**pounds brussels sprouts, shaved or shredded**

Season the chicken breasts with 1½ teaspoons of the salt and the pepper.

In a cast-iron skillet over medium heat, heat the olive oil and the butter. When the fat is hot, add the chicken breasts and cook, undisturbed, for 4 to 5 minutes to create a "crust" on the chicken. Flip the chicken and spoon some of the fat from the pan over the top. Cook the chicken for 4 to 5 minutes more, until browned on the second side. Flip the chicken again and spoon some of the fat from the pan over the top. Cover the skillet and cook until the internal temperature of the chicken reaches 165°F. (Use your instant-read thermometer to check.) Transfer the chicken to a platter and cover it loosely with aluminum foil.

Add the brussels sprouts and the remaining ½ teaspoon salt to the chicken drippings in the pan and increase the heat to medium-high. Cook, stirring, for 3 to 4 minutes, until the brussels sprouts start to soften. Reduce the heat to medium and cook until the brussels sprouts are tender and lightly crisped, 2 to 3 minutes more.

To serve, slice the chicken and serve it on top of the brussels sprouts. Store any leftovers in separate airtight containers in the refrigerator for up to 3 days.

Chile-Lime Plantains

SERVES
6 TO 8

Dairy-Free

Gluten-Free

Grain-Free

Nut-Free

Paleo

Vegan

Vegetarian

I never knew just how delicious and easy fried plantains, a.k.a. tostones, could be. You'll want to employ the "double-fry" technique to get them extra crispy. Serve them with your favorite dip or alongside tacos.

¼ cup chile-lime seasoning, such as Tajín or Trader Joe's Chile Lime Seasoning Blend

2 teaspoons salt

4 green plantains, peeled

¼ cup coconut oil
   Cilantro-Jalapeño Aïoli
   (page 28; optional)

Cover a sturdy cutting board with several layers of paper towels.

Combine the chile-lime seasoning and salt in a bowl. Set it aside.

Slice the plantains into ½-inch-thick discs. In a large skillet or Dutch oven over medium heat, melt the coconut oil. When the oil is hot, working in batches, add the plantains and cook them for 2 to 3 minutes on each side, until they are tender. Using a slotted spoon, transfer them to the lined cutting board to drain.

When all the plantain slices have been cooked, lightly smash them with the flat side of a meat tenderizer into flat discs. Again, working in batches, return the flattened plantains to the hot oil and fry until they are lightly browned and crisped, 2 to 3 minutes on each side. Using the slotted spoon, remove them from the oil and immediately dredge them in the chile-lime salt. Set them on a wire rack to cool while you fry the remaining plantain slices.

Serve alone or with Cilantro-Jalapeño Aïoli, if desired.

Caramelized Cherries and Yogurt

I don't always plan for a sweet treat after dinner but often find myself wishing I had. Thankfully, this recipe is easy enough to whip up at a moment's notice to satisfy any last-minute cravings. It's quickly become one of my favorites and sure to be one of yours. With just three main ingredients, it's amazing how much flavor you can get in this delightful dessert. The sweet, syrupy cherries paired with the cool, tart, thick Greek yogurt will leave you wanting more. And more. And more. This recipe will make enough for two, but if you eat it all yourself, I promise I won't tell anyone.

SERVES 2

Gluten-Free
Grain-Free
Nut-Free
Vegetarian

3 **cups pitted fresh or thawed frozen dark sweet cherries**

¼ **cup honey**

2½ **to 3 tablespoons bourbon**

1½ **cups plain whole-milk Greek yogurt**

Combine the cherries, honey, bourbon, and ¼ cup water in a medium saucepan and cook over medium-high heat, stirring frequently and lightly breaking up the cherries with a fork as they cook, for 10 minutes.

Reduce the heat to medium and simmer, stirring occasionally, for 10 minutes more, until the cherries have broken down further and the syrup is thick and caramel-y. Remove from the heat and let cool slightly.

To serve, divide the yogurt between two bowls and spoon the cherries and syrup over the top.

chapter 5

one-dish wonders

ONE POT. One baking dish. One Dutch oven. One pan. Whatever it is you're cooking your food in, you need just one of them for the recipes in this chapter.

And you know what that means? Just one cooking vessel to clean. Hallelujah.

We focus so much on how time-consuming meal prep can be that we often forget how long the cleanup can take. As someone who hates doing dishes, I love when a recipe doesn't involve having to clean a million dishes when it's done.

For these recipes, you'll simply need one pot, some measuring utensils, a knife, and a cutting board.

119	Chai-Spiced Kettle-Style Apples
120	Ranchero Skillet Breakfast Tacos
123	Summer Corn Chowder
126	Black Bean Soup
129	Salmon Curry
131	Grain-Free Crispy Honey Shrimp and Bok Choy
135	Sun-Dried Tomato and Goat Cheese Frittata
136	Cauliflower Rice Paella
139	Artichoke and Kalamata Cod
141	Beverly's Chicken Adobo
143	Garam Masala Rice and Apricots

Chai-Spiced Kettle-Style Apples

SERVES 6

Gluten-Free

Grain-Free

Nut-Free

Paleo

Vegan

Vegetarian

Traditional applesauce makes me think of kids and root canal patients. Kettle-cooked apples, on the other hand? That makes me think of a glamorous starlet casually lounging on her all-white bed in a fancy Beverly Hills hotel. Okay, fine. It's not that. But it's not like boring ol' applesauce, either. This recipe is like the cooler big sister applesauce never knew it wanted. Add a pinch of chai spice, and you have yourself a proper adult treat. Whether you eat it as is by the forkful or use it to top a bowl of ice cream or a stack of pancakes is entirely up to you.

5 Gala apples, peeled, cored, and sliced into ½-inch-thick wedges

1½ teaspoons Chai Spice Blend (page 16)

⅓ cup pure maple syrup

1 tablespoon fresh lemon juice

1½ tablespoons butter or ghee

1 teaspoon pure vanilla extract

1 teaspoon tapioca flour

Combine the apples and chai spice in a stockpot or Dutch oven. Use a wooden spoon to stir the apples and coat them evenly with the spices. Add the maple syrup, lemon juice, butter, and vanilla and stir to combine. Cook over medium heat, stirring occasionally, until the apples have softened, 7 to 8 minutes.

Push the apples to one side of the pot and slowly sprinkle the tapioca flour over the liquid pooled on the open side of the pot. Whisk the tapioca into the liquid to create a slurry and thicken the liquid. Once the tapioca is well combined, stir in the apples to coat them in the thickened syrup.

Serve hot, warm, at room temperature, or cold. Store leftovers in an airtight container in the refrigerator for up to 5 days.

tips: *If you don't have chai spice on hand or don't feel like making the Chai Spice Blend, feel free to substitute 1½ teaspoons ground cinnamon. But really, just make the Chai Spice Blend. No Gala apples on hand? Granny Smiths and Honeycrisps make great alternatives.*

Ranchero Skillet Breakfast Tacos

MAKES 8
TACOS

Gluten-Free

*Grain-Free
(option)*

Nut-Free

Breakfast tacos that can be made in a jiffy in one dish? Don't worry, it's not a dream. It's Ranchero Skillet Breakfast Tacos!

1 teaspoon extra-virgin olive oil

½ medium sweet onion, chopped

½ red bell pepper, chopped

2 teaspoons salt

½ pound ground beef

6 large eggs

2 tablespoons canned diced green chiles

2 tablespoons light coconut milk

½ cup shredded pepper Jack cheese

8 corn tortillas or grain-free tortillas (see Tip)

⅓ cup chopped fresh cilantro

Hot sauce of your choice, for serving

tip: Use grain-free tortillas, such as from Siete Family, to make these grain-free. If you'd prefer not to serve these as tacos, simply omit the tortillas for a delicious scramble. Top with cilantro and hot sauce and enjoy.

In a cast-iron skillet over medium heat, heat the olive oil. When the oil is hot, add the onion, bell pepper, and ½ teaspoon of the salt. Cook, stirring occasionally, for 7 to 8 minutes, until the vegetables are tender and lightly browned on the edges. Push the vegetables to the side of the pan. Add the ground beef and ½ teaspoon of the salt to the pan and cook, gently breaking up the beef with a wooden spoon as it cooks, until the beef is browned, 8 to 10 minutes. Stir the vegetables from the side of the pan into the beef to combine.

Whisk the eggs lightly. Add the green chiles, coconut milk, and remaining 1 teaspoon salt and whisk to combine. Pour the eggs into the skillet and let sit for about 30 seconds. When the eggs start to form curds, gently stir them, folding them over themselves and combining them with the other ingredients. Then, when the eggs are no longer runny, add the cheese and fold it in. Cook for 1 minute more, until the cheese has melted and the eggs are cooked through.

Divide the tortillas among 4 plates (2 each). Top each tortilla with the egg mixture and sprinkle with cilantro and hot sauce. Take a giant bite and enjoy.

Summer Corn Chowder

SERVES
4 TO 6

Gluten-Free
Grain-Free
Nut-Free
Paleo

When I lived in San Francisco, Ami, my darling and hilarious roommate at the time, used to make an amazing corn chowder. I loved that dang soup! She made a lot of amazing food, but this dish always stood out. Here's the thing, though: It was made with cream, and all that cream just doesn't sit well with my stomach the way it used to. So I made a few simple modifications to her recipe, and voilà! My stomach is happy again and I can eat all the chowder I desire.

Because this recipe works better with fresh corn, a summer staple, I add a few summery ingredients such as fresh basil and tomatoes. It's a perfect combination, and yes, you can still have soup in the summer. Just let it cool a bit before digging in!

4 ears corn, husked

6 tablespoons butter or ghee

1 yellow onion, chopped

2½ teaspoons salt

3 celery stalks, chopped

2 red bell peppers, diced

1 large jalapeño, seeds and ribs removed, minced

3 garlic cloves, minced

2 teaspoons freshly ground black pepper

½ teaspoon smoked paprika

⅛ teaspoon cayenne pepper

3 tablespoons tapioca flour

4 cups chicken broth

1 (13.5- to 14-ounce) can full-fat coconut milk (see Tip)

⅓ cup chopped fresh basil

1 cup cherry tomatoes, halved

Fill a large pot with 2 to 3 inches of water and bring to a boil. Insert a steamer basket and add the corn. Cover the pot and steam the corn for 6 to 7 minutes, until the corn is tender and easily pierced with a fork. Remove the corn from the pot and set aside to cool. When the corn is cool enough to handle, cut the kernels from the cobs using a sharp knife and put them in a bowl. Set the corn aside.

Pour the water out of the pot, add 4 tablespoons of the butter, and melt over medium heat. When the butter is hot, add the onion and 1 teaspoon of the salt. Cook until the onion is soft and translucent, 7 to 8 minutes. Add the celery, bell peppers, jalapeño, and 1 teaspoon of the salt. Cook, stirring occasionally, until the celery and bell peppers are soft, 5 to 6 minutes. Add the garlic, black pepper, paprika, and cayenne and cook for 1 minute more.

Meanwhile, in a small microwave-safe bowl, melt the remaining 2 tablespoons butter in the microwave. While

continues

ONE-DISH WONDERS

xo

Summer Corn Chowder, <u>continued</u>

whisking continuously, slowly sprinkle the tapioca flour over the butter and whisk until well combined to create a quick roux.

Add the broth and coconut milk to the pot. While stirring, slowly drizzle the roux into the soup and stir until incorporated. Add the corn kernels and the remaining ½ teaspoon salt. Reduce the heat to low and simmer the soup for 5 to 7 minutes.

To serve, divide the soup among four to six bowls and sprinkle the basil and tomatoes over the top. Store any leftover soup in an airtight container in the refrigerator for up to 5 days.

tip: If you don't like coconut, are allergic to it, or would just prefer to use traditional dairy, whole milk can be substituted for the coconut milk. And this recipe is just as decadent using ghee in place of the butter.

Black Bean Soup

**SERVES
6 TO 8**

Dairy-Free

Gluten-Free

Grain-Free

Nut-Free

*Vegan
(option)*

*Vegetarian
(option)*

When I think "black bean soup," I think bold flavors. Oftentimes that also means spicy, which in turn means my kids won't eat it. I designed this soup to have bold flavors that we adults can appreciate but without the spice, so the kids can indulge sans complaining.

4   slices bacon, chopped (see Tip)

1   yellow onion, chopped

2½ teaspoons salt

1   poblano pepper, finely chopped

1   red bell pepper, chopped

2   teaspoons smoked paprika

1   teaspoon chili powder

4   garlic cloves, minced

3   (15-ounce) cans black beans,
    with their liquid

1   (14.5-ounce) can diced
    tomatoes, with their juices

2   cups chicken broth

    Juice of 1 lime (about
    2 tablespoons)

¼   cup chopped fresh cilantro

1   cup cherry tomatoes, halved

Heat a large stockpot or Dutch oven over medium heat. Add the bacon and cook, stirring frequently, until the bacon is lightly crisped and browned, 7 to 8 minutes. Remove the bacon from the pot with a slotted spoon and set it aside on a paper towel–lined plate to drain.

Add the onion and ½ teaspoon of the salt to the bacon fat and cook until the onion is tender and lightly browned, 8 to 9 minutes. Add the poblano, bell pepper, paprika, and chili powder and cook, stirring occasionally, until the peppers are soft, 5 to 6 minutes. Add the garlic and cook for 1 minute more. Add the beans and their liquid, tomatoes, broth, lime juice, and remaining 2 teaspoons salt and bring to a simmer. Simmer the soup, uncovered, for 10 minutes.

Carefully transfer 2 cups of the soup to a blender and blend on high speed for about 10 seconds to puree it. Return the pureed soup to the pot, stir in the bacon, cover, and simmer for 5 minutes more.

To serve, divide the soup among six to eight bowls and top with the cilantro and cherry tomatoes.

tip: If you'd like to make this recipe for vegan or vegetarian friends, simply omit the bacon, cook the onion in 2 teaspoons avocado oil, and swap in vegetable broth for the chicken broth.

Salmon Curry

Not too long ago, my friend Teresa asked if I could re-create a salmon curry dish she'd had somewhere. She gave me a rundown of what she remembered to be in the recipe: "It was yellow curry and had salmon." With no other description, I had my marching orders. Having never tried the curry dish and without even knowing what the full ingredient list was, I set about trying to create the best damn yellow salmon curry I possibly could. Whether this tastes like the dish she had in mind or not, I have no idea. But I do know it's damn delicious and will knock your socks off. My immodest self is going to say it's probably even better than the original. But that would be obnoxious, so I won't say it. Since this curry reheats so well, the recipe makes a large batch. Plan to have leftovers, or invite your friends over! Serve this over cauliflower rice or plain white rice.

SERVES 6 TO 8

Dairy-Free
Gluten-Free
Grain-Free
Nut-Free
Paleo

1½ **pounds salmon fillet**

4½ **teaspoons salt**

¼ **teaspoon freshly ground black pepper**

1 **tablespoon plus 1 teaspoon coconut oil**

1 **sweet onion, chopped**

2 **carrots, sliced**

1 **red bell pepper, sliced**

½ **pound French green beans (haricots verts), trimmed**

3 **cups full-fat coconut milk**

½ **cup coconut cream (see Tip)**

½ **cup chicken broth**

2 **tablespoons coconut sugar**

2 **tablespoons curry powder**

1 **teaspoon fish sauce**

Cooked rice or Oven-Roasted Cauliflower Rice (page 73), for serving

Season the salmon fillet evenly with 2 teaspoons of the salt and the pepper. In a Dutch oven or large pot over medium heat, melt 1 tablespoon of the coconut oil. When the oil is hot, add the salmon, skin-side down. Cook until the salmon is cooked through and flakes easily with a fork, 3 to 4 minutes on each side. Transfer the salmon to a plate and set aside.

Add the remaining 1 teaspoon coconut oil, the onion, and ½ teaspoon of the salt to the pot. Cook until the onion is tender, 6 to 7 minutes. Add the carrots and

continues

Salmon Curry, continued

cook for 3 to 4 minutes. Add the bell pepper and green beans and cook until all the vegetables are tender, 3 to 4 minutes more.

Add the coconut milk, coconut cream, broth, coconut sugar, curry powder, fish sauce, and remaining 2 teaspoons salt and stir to combine. Remove and discard the skin from the salmon. Break the salmon into large chunks and add it to the pot. Bring the curry to a light simmer and simmer until the salmon is heated through, about 5 minutes.

To serve, spoon the curry over rice or cauliflower rice. Store any leftovers in an airtight container in the refrigerator for up to 4 days.

tip: *You can purchase coconut cream or make it easily at home. Simply put a can of full-fat coconut milk in the refrigerator overnight. As the coconut milk chills, the coconut cream rises to the top and solidifies. When you open the can, you can see that the coconut milk has separated into coconut water and luscious coconut cream. Scrape out the cream and use it as directed. Feel free to reserve the coconut water, refrigerated in an airtight container, to add to smoothies or other beverages at a later date.*

Grain-Free Crispy Honey Shrimp and Bok Choy

SERVES 4

Dairy-Free
Gluten-Free
Grain-Free
Nut-Free
Paleo

While this recipe can indeed serve four, if your family is anything like mine, you may need to double-batch it, because you are certain to want to go back for seconds. It's *that* tasty!

1 **pound raw medium shrimp, peeled (tails removed) and deveined**

3½ **teaspoons salt**

¼ **cup One-Minute Mayo (page 35)**

2 **tablespoons honey**

¼ **teaspoon cayenne pepper**

3 **large egg whites**

½ **cup tapioca flour**

2 **tablespoons coconut oil, plus more if needed**

½ **pound cremini mushrooms, sliced**

8 **baby bok choy, chopped**

2 **tablespoons coconut aminos**

Season the shrimp with 1½ teaspoons of the salt and set aside. Line a plate with several layers of paper towels and place it near the stovetop.

Combine the mayonnaise, honey, and ⅛ teaspoon of the cayenne in a large bowl and stir well. Set aside.

Put the egg whites in another large bowl and whisk until frothy, about 1 minute. Add the tapioca flour, ½ teaspoon of the salt, and the remaining ⅛ teaspoon cayenne and whisk until the batter is smooth. Add the shrimp and stir to make sure they are well coated.

In a large skillet over medium-high heat, melt the coconut oil. When the oil is hot, working in batches, use a slotted spoon to remove the shrimp from the batter and carefully place them in the oil. Fry until they are cooked through and the batter is a light golden brown, 2 to 3 minutes on each side. Using a slotted spoon, transfer the shrimp to the paper towel–lined plate to drain. Cover the plate of shrimp loosely with aluminum foil to keep warm. Repeat to fry the remaining shrimp,

continues

**Grain-Free Crispy Honey Shrimp
and Bok Choy, <u>continued</u>**

adding more coconut oil to the pan between batches if it goes dry while frying.

When the shrimp are all cooked, add the mushrooms and ½ teaspoon of the salt to the skillet. Cook, stirring occasionally, until the mushrooms are tender, 5 to 7 minutes. Add the bok choy, the remaining 1 teaspoon salt, and the coconut aminos and cook, stirring, until the vegetables are tender, 5 to 6 minutes.

Add the cooked shrimp to the honey-mayonnaise sauce and stir them gently to coat evenly.

Serve the braised bok choy and mushrooms alongside the honey shrimp.

Sun-Dried Tomato and Goat Cheese Frittata

SERVES
4 TO 6

Gluten-Free

Grain-Free

Nut-Free

I bet you thought sun-dried tomatoes went out in the '90s. Remember when *everything* was sun-dried tomatoes back then? Well, they're back! And better than ever, as evidenced by this recipe.

While frittatas are traditionally known as a breakfast food, we often have them for dinner over here. They're incredibly easy to whip up on a busy evening, and the leftovers transition to a perfect breakfast the next morning.

2	teaspoons extra-virgin olive oil
½	sweet onion, chopped
1	teaspoon salt
10	large eggs
¼	cup light coconut milk or coconut milk beverage
½	cup sliced sun-dried tomatoes
3	ounces soft goat cheese, crumbled (about ¾ cup)
	Freshly ground black pepper
	Chopped fresh flat-leaf parsley, for garnish (optional)

Preheat the oven to 350°F.

Heat a large oven-safe nonstick skillet over medium heat and add the olive oil. When the oil is hot, add the onion and ½ teaspoon of the salt. Cook, stirring occasionally, until the onion is tender and lightly browned, 7 to 8 minutes.

Whisk together the eggs, coconut milk, and remaining ½ teaspoon salt in a medium bowl until well combined. Add the eggs and sun-dried tomatoes to the skillet with the onion and use a spatula to slowly stir the eggs for 30 seconds, creating large curds. Sprinkle the goat cheese over the top and season with pepper. Transfer the pan to the oven and bake for 8 to 9 minutes, until the eggs are no longer runny. Remove the frittata from the oven and let cool for 5 minutes.

Cut the frittata into 8 wedges, garnish with chopped parsley, if desired, and serve. Store any leftovers in an airtight container in the refrigerator for up to 5 days.

xo

135

Cauliflower Rice Paella

GREAT for LEFTOVERS

My Spanish grandmother may be rolling in her grave this very moment at the thought that I've destroyed her traditional paella recipe. But the truth is, a traditional paella is time-intensive and can include ingredients like rabbit, escargot, or mussels. While the ingredients and techniques vary by region, paella can take a bit of time and use some ingredients you may not be accustomed to, so you're less likely to incorporate it into your meal plans. But the flavors are out of this world and should not be missed. I decided to simplify the cooking techniques a bit and use ingredients everyone is certain to be familiar with. I also swapped out the rice for cauliflower to get some veggies in.

SERVES 6

Dairy-Free

Gluten-Free

Grain-Free

Nut-Free

4   boneless, skinless chicken thighs (about 1 pound)

3   teaspoons salt

¼   teaspoon freshly ground black pepper

½   pound raw medium shrimp, peeled and deveined

3   teaspoons extra-virgin olive oil

1   yellow onion, chopped

1   pound fresh (Mexican) chorizo, casings removed

3 cloves garlic, minced

1   (15-ounce) can crushed tomatoes

1   cup chicken broth

⅓   cup white wine (whatever you have on hand will work; I prefer a dry white)

1   tablespoon fresh lemon juice

2   teaspoons smoked paprika

2   pinches of saffron threads (see Tip)

1   pound cauliflower rice, homemade (from 1 small head) or store-bought

¼   cup chopped fresh flat-leaf parsley, for garnish

Season the chicken thighs with 1 teaspoon of the salt and the pepper. Season the shrimp with ½ teaspoon of the salt.

In a paella pan or Dutch oven over medium heat, heat 2 teaspoons of the olive oil. When the oil is hot, add the chicken thighs. Cook on one side until lightly browned, 3 to 4 minutes. Flip the chicken and cook for 3 minutes on the second side, then push the chicken to one side of the pan. Add the shrimp and cook until they are cooked through and light pink, 2 to 3 minutes per side. Remove the chicken and shrimp from the pan and set both aside.

continues

Cauliflower Rice Paella, <u>continued</u>

Add the remaining 1 teaspoon olive oil to the pan. When the oil is hot, add the onion and ½ teaspoon of the salt. Cook until the onion is soft and translucent, 6 to 7 minutes. Push the onion to the side of the pan and add the chorizo. Cook, using a wooden spoon to break up the chorizo as it cooks, until it's lightly browned and cooked through, 5 to 6 minutes.

Add the garlic and cook, stirring frequently, for about 1 minute. Add the tomatoes, broth, wine, lemon juice, paprika, saffron, cauliflower rice, and remaining 1 teaspoon salt, stir, and bring everything to a simmer. Simmer for 15 to 20 minutes, until the cauliflower rice is tender. Depending on the size of the pieces of cauliflower, the time will vary, so make sure to check for doneness early.

Return the shrimp and chicken to the pan and cook to heat them through, 3 minutes more.

Sprinkle the parsley over the top and serve.

tip: *If you don't have saffron, that's okay; the recipe is still delicious without it!*

Artichoke and Kalamata Cod

Dairy-Free

Gluten-Free

Grain-Free

Nut-Free

Paleo

This dinner may just be the easiest recipe in this book. In fact, it's taking me longer to figure out what to say about it than it takes to make it. It's easy. It's delicious. And anyone can make it. It's what this cookbook is all about.

- 1 **pound skinless cod fillets**
- 1½ **teaspoons salt**
- ⅛ **teaspoon lemon pepper**
- 1 **cup marinated artichoke hearts, drained**
- ½ **cup pitted kalamata olives**
- 2 **tablespoons capers, drained**

Preheat the oven to 400°F.

Season the cod fillets with the salt and lemon pepper.

Spread the artichokes and olives over the bottom of a 9 by 13-inch baking dish. Nestle the cod fillets among the vegetables and sprinkle the capers over the top. Bake for about 15 minutes, until the cod is cooked through and flakes easily with a fork.

To serve, plate the cod, then arrange the vegetables over or around it.

Beverly's Chicken Adobo

GREAT
for
LEFTOVERS

**SERVES
4 TO 6**

Dairy-Free

Gluten-Free

*Grain-Free
(option)*

Nut-Free

*Paleo
(option)*

My dear friend Beverly and I have been friends since we were five, from our early days of Hello Kitty and New Kids On The Block right up until now, when my kids refuse to listen to New Kids On The Block because they think they "aren't cool anymore." Whatever. They're still cool to us (#donnieandjordan4ever). One of the things Beverly and I connect over today (other than aging boy bands) is our love for cooking. I'll cook for her, she'll cook for me, and sometimes we'll cook together. A while back, she had me over for dinner and made a modified version of the chicken adobo she grew up eating. It was always her favorite dish growing up and I instantly understood why. I couldn't stop eating it. I went back for thirds and ate an embarrassing amount of food that day. Beverly modified the original recipe by swapping in coconut aminos for soy sauce, a cleaner alternative. And the night she came over to teach me how to make this? It was gobbled up! The kids had seconds, Brad had seconds, it was gone. She so kindly agreed to share her recipe so that you, too, can eat like a maniac and go for thirds. If you'd like to follow Beverly and her food journey, you can find her on Instagram, @thepetitepanaderya.

2¼ pounds boneless, skinless chicken thighs (see Tip)

2 teaspoons salt

½ teaspoon freshly ground black pepper

2 teaspoons extra-virgin olive oil

6 garlic cloves, minced

1 cup coconut aminos

1 cup unseasoned rice vinegar

1 bay leaf

5 Yukon Gold potatoes (about 1½ pounds), cut into 1-inch cubes

2 cups cooked white rice or Oven-Roasted Cauliflower Rice (page 73), for serving

Season the chicken thighs with the salt and pepper.

In a Dutch oven over medium heat, heat the olive oil. When the oil is hot, add the garlic and cook, stirring, for 1 minute. Add the chicken thighs and cook until lightly browned, 3 to 4 minutes on each side.

Add the coconut aminos, vinegar, and bay leaf. Nestle the potatoes among the chicken so they are submerged

continues

xo

Beverly's Chicken Adobo, <u>continued</u>

in the liquid. Cover the pot, bring the liquid to a low boil, and cook for about 10 minutes.

Uncover the pot, flip the chicken pieces, and nestle the potatoes into the liquid again. Cover and cook for 10 minutes more.

Remove the lid, flip the chicken, and tuck in the potatoes again. Simmer, uncovered, for 20 minutes more. Remove the bay leaf.

Serve over white rice or cauliflower rice.

tip: *You can also use bone-on, skin-on chicken thighs in this recipe.*

Garam Masala Rice and Apricots

For such a simple recipe, it's amazing how many flavors are packed into this rice dish. And it's a great recipe to make a batch of to reheat through the week.

**SERVES
4 TO 6**

*Dairy-Free
(option)*

*Vegan
(option)*

Vegetarian

2 tablespoons butter or ghee (see Tip)

½ sweet onion, chopped

1 teaspoon salt

4 cups cooked white rice

1 teaspoon garam masala

½ cup chopped dried apricots

½ cup slivered almonds

1 tablespoon chopped fresh mint

1 tablespoon chopped fresh flat-leaf parsley

In a cast-iron skillet over medium heat, melt the butter. When the butter is hot, add the onion and ½ teaspoon of the salt. Cook until the onion is tender and lightly browned, 7 to 8 minutes.

Push the onion to one side of the skillet and add the rice. Cook, letting the rice crisp up until it gets a light crust on the bottom, 2 to 3 minutes. Add the remaining ½ teaspoon salt, the garam masala, apricots, and almonds and stir to combine. Remove from the heat.

Sprinkle the mint and parsley over the top and serve. Store any leftovers in an airtight container in the refrigerator for up to 5 days.

tip: *To make this dairy free, swap the butter for ghee. To make this vegan, swap the butter or ghee for extra-virgin olive oil.*

chapter 6

30 minutes or less

I DON'T KNOW ABOUT YOU, but between work, kids' soccer practice, homework (theirs, not mine), and life in general, weekdays can get a little hairy around here. The last thing I feel like doing is moseying around the kitchen cooking.

And I love cooking! But not when I have a million other things going on. I need something quick to whip up Monday through Friday. And damn, it better be delicious. Because how great is it to look forward to a delicious meal, dessert, or snack at the end of the day?

The recipes in this chapter are designed to get food on the table *fast*. Whether you need a quick recipe to feed your hungry family or you have some last-minute guests popping by, you're covered.

147	Grain-Free Fish Sticks and Tartar Sauce
149	Seared Ahi and Cabbage
153	Drive-Through Burger Bowls
154	Italian Sub Skewers
157	Harissa-Spiced Cauliflower Fritters
158	Haloumi and Watermelon Skewers
161	Asian Chicken Patties with Braised Bok Choy and Cabbage
162	Greek Meatballs, Cukes, and Tzatziki
167	Chorizo-Stuffed Dates
168	Pan-Seared Salmon with Dill and Sautéed Spinach
171	California Caprese
172	Pesto Shrimp and Cauli Puree
175	Burrata, Peach, and Blood Orange Salad

Grain-Free Fish Sticks and Tartar Sauce

Ahhh, fish sticks. I have such mixed feelings about fish sticks. I mean, I'm a child of the '80s, when frozen fish sticks were a staple on so many dinner tables. We can all picture and smell them still. For better or worse. I loved those frozen processed fish sticks back then. Now? Not so much.

But I *do* love fresh fish and anything battered and fried, so I knew I needed to reinvent the fish sticks of my youth into ones I could feel good about giving my kids today. And here they are! I even included a quick little clean tartar sauce to serve alongside them. If you want to give your kids the full '80s experience, serve them up with some ketchup. Either way, they'll love them.

SERVES 4 TO 6

Dairy-Free

Gluten-Free

Grain-Free

Paleo

TARTAR SAUCE

- ½ cup One-Minute Mayo (page 35)
- 1 teaspoon sweet pickle relish
- ½ teaspoon yellow mustard
- ½ teaspoon fresh lemon juice
- ¼ teaspoon dried dill
  Salt

FISH STICKS

- 2 pounds skinless cod fillets, cut into 5 by 2-inch "sticks"
- 3 teaspoons salt, plus more as needed
- 1½ cups almond flour
- ¼ cup plus 2 tablespoons tapioca flour
- ½ teaspoon garlic powder
- 2 large eggs
- ½ cup coconut oil

To make the tartar sauce: Stir together the mayonnaise, relish, mustard, lemon juice, and dill in a small bowl. Season with salt and set aside.

To make the fish sticks: Season the cod with 2 teaspoons of the salt. Combine the almond flour, tapioca flour, garlic powder, and remaining 1 teaspoon salt in a large bowl. Beat the eggs in a medium bowl.

continues

**Grain-Free Fish Sticks and Tartar Sauce,
continued**

Dredge the cod in the beaten eggs, letting the excess drip off, then roll in the flour mixture to coat completely. Set the fish sticks on a wire rack.

Line a plate with paper towels and place it near the stovetop.

In a large skillet or Dutch oven over medium heat, melt the coconut oil. When the oil is hot, working in batches, add the fish sticks to the skillet and fry until the crust is a light golden brown and the fish is cooked through, 2 to 3 minutes per side. Transfer the cooked fish sticks to the paper towel–lined plate to drain and season with salt.

Serve the fish sticks with the tartar sauce on the side.

tip: While frying the fish sticks, make sure to flip the fish gently so as not to tear off the batter. Grain-free batters tend to be a little more delicate than their heartier gluten-y counterparts.

Seared Ahi and Cabbage

You are going to flip when you realize you can whip up this tasty lunch or dinner in under thirty minutes. In fact, you can probably whip it up in about fifteen, if I'm being honest. Not only that, but you're going to feel like you're having dinner at your favorite sushi spot, except you'll be in the comfort of your own home, in your slippers, makeup off, with a messy bun . . . or maybe that's just me. Either way, this one is going to be in regular rotation for you, mark my words.

**SERVES
4 TO 6**

Dairy-Free

Gluten-Free

Grain-Free

Nut-Free

AHI AND CABBAGE

- 2 pounds ahi tuna steaks
- 2 teaspoons salt
- ¼ teaspoon freshly ground black pepper
- ¼ cup coconut aminos
- 2 tablespoons plus 1 teaspoon toasted sesame oil
- 1 tablespoon plus 1 teaspoon tamari (see Tip)
- 4 garlic cloves, minced
- 2 teaspoons sriracha
- 1 teaspoon fresh ginger, grated on a Microplane
- 1 teaspoon unseasoned rice vinegar
- 4 green onions, light green and white parts only, thinly sliced
- 3 cups coleslaw mix
- 2 teaspoons avocado oil

SRIRACHA MAYO

- ⅓ cup One-Minute Mayo (page 35)
- 1 tablespoon sriracha
- ½ teaspoon fresh lime juice
- ¼ teaspoon salt
- 1 garlic clove, minced
- 1 green onion (light green and white parts only), sliced, for serving
- 1 tablespoon chopped fresh cilantro, for serving

To start the ahi: Season all sides of the ahi steaks with the salt and pepper and set them aside.

To make the cabbage: Whisk together the coconut aminos, sesame oil, tamari, garlic, sriracha, ginger,

continues

Seared Ahi and Cabbage,
<u>continued</u>

vinegar, and green onions in a large bowl. Add the coleslaw mix and mix well to coat. Set aside.

In a cast-iron skillet over medium-high heat, heat the avocado oil. When the oil is hot, add the ahi steaks and sear them until golden brown on the outside but still pink inside, 1 to 2 minutes on each side.

To make the sriracha mayo: Combine the mayonnaise, sriracha, lime juice, salt, and garlic in a small bowl and stir to combine.

To serve, plate the cabbage and top it with the seared ahi. Sprinkle the sliced green onion and cilantro over the top and serve with the sriracha mayo on the side.

tip: If you'd like to omit the tamari from the recipe, simply substitute more coconut aminos and season with salt at the end.

Drive-Through Burger Bowls

SERVES 4

Dairy-Free
Gluten-Free
Grain-Free
Nut-Free
Paleo

If you live in California, you most certainly know what this burger bowl is attempting to re-create. If you need a hint, it rhymes with "Min-N-Mout Manimal-Style" burgers. However! It's a version you can enjoy at home in less than thirty minutes. Which, truth be told, may be even quicker than leaving your house and sitting in line at the drive-through.

SAUCE

- ½ cup One-Minute Mayo (page 35)
- 1½ tablespoons sweet pickle relish
- 2 teaspoons tomato paste
- 1 teaspoon yellow mustard
- ½ teaspoon salt

BURGER BOWLS

- 2 teaspoons extra-virgin olive oil
- 1 medium sweet onion, finely chopped
- 2 teaspoons salt
- 1 pound ground beef
- 1 head iceberg lettuce, chopped
- 1 cup dill pickle slices
- 1 cup cherry tomatoes, halved

To make the sauce: Combine the mayonnaise, relish, tomato paste, mustard, and salt in a small bowl and stir well. Set aside.

To make the burger bowls: In a large skillet over medium heat, heat 1 teaspoon of the olive oil. When the oil is hot, add the onion and ¾ teaspoon of the salt. Cook, stirring occasionally, until the onion is tender and browned, 9 to 10 minutes. Remove the onion from the pan and set aside.

Add the remaining 1 teaspoon olive oil, the ground beef, and the remaining 1¼ teaspoons salt to the pan. Cook, using a wooden spoon to break up the beef as it cooks, until it is browned and cooked through, 7 to 9 minutes.

To serve the burger bowls, divide the lettuce evenly among four bowls and top each with one-quarter of the ground beef, one-quarter of the dill pickles, and one-quarter of the tomatoes. Drizzle with the sauce and serve.

tip: If you'd like the authentic drive-through experience, place a slice of American cheese on top of the ground beef immediately after plating it, while it is still hot. There are better-for-you versions of American cheese available at some natural food stores.

Italian Sub Skewers

MAKES 12
SKEWERS

Gluten-Free

Grain-Free

Nut-Free

If you ever find yourself scrambling for a last-minute appetizer to serve guests or to bring along to an event (like me, every time), scramble no further! This handy party app is a crowd-pleaser and loved by procrastinators everywhere.

12 **slices prosciutto, cut crosswise in half**

24 **slices salami**

24 **kalamata olives, pitted**

12 **pepperoncini**

12 **bite-size mozzarella balls (*ciliegini*)**

2 **red bell peppers, cut into 24 squares total**

4 **ounces provolone cheese, cut into 12 cubes**

In whatever order you like, thread 2 pieces of prosciutto, 2 salami slices, 2 olives, 1 pepperoncini, 1 mozzarella ball, 2 bell pepper squares, and 1 provolone cube onto each of twelve 6-inch wooden skewers. Feel free to mix up the pattern on each. Serve immediately or pack into an airtight storage container and bring it along with you to a party.

Harissa-Spiced Cauliflower Fritters

MAKES
ABOUT 14
FRITTERS

Dairy-Free

Gluten-Free

Grain-Free

Vegetarian

Fritters are such a great way to get your vegetables in. Especially into your kids! The fritter batter will be slightly loose but will fry up to the perfect consistency.

About 6 cups cauliflower florets (1½ pounds)

½ **cup tapioca flour**

½ **cup almond flour**

½ **cup crushed pork rinds (chicharrónes)**

¼ **cup harissa**

1 **tablespoon chopped fresh flat-leaf parsley**

6 **Medjool dates, pitted and chopped into small pieces**

3 **large eggs, beaten**

2½ **teaspoons salt, plus more as needed**

½ **teaspoon freshly ground black pepper**

¼ **cup coconut oil, plus more if needed**

tip: To keep their shape intact, I find it easier to use a spatula to slide the cauliflower fritters into the hot oil.

Fill a large pot with 2 to 3 inches of water and bring to a boil. Insert a steamer basket in the pot and add the cauliflower florets. Cover the pot and steam the cauliflower for 6 to 7 minutes, until fork-tender but not mushy. Remove the basket from the pot and let the cauliflower cool to the touch.

Chop the cauliflower into small pieces about the size of black beans. Put the cauliflower in a large bowl and add the tapioca flour, almond flour, pork rinds, harissa, parsley, dates, eggs, salt, and pepper. Use your hands to combine everything thoroughly.

Line a plate with paper towels and place it near the stovetop.

In a large skillet over medium heat, melt the coconut oil. When the oil is hot, working in batches, scoop about 2 tablespoons of the cauliflower mixture into your hand and form it into a patty. Add the patties to the oil (see Tip) and fry until golden brown, 3 to 4 minutes on each side. Transfer the fritters to the paper towel–lined plate to drain. Immediately season with salt and serve. Repeat to fry the remaining fritters, adding more coconut oil between batches if the pan looks dry.

xo

Halloumi and Watermelon Skewers

MAKES 6
SKEWERS

Gluten-Free

Grain-Free

Nut-Free

Vegetarian

Halloumi is a cheese from Cyprus that is often grilled because it holds its shape well when exposed to heat. If you're someone who likes to pick the crispy bits from a casserole pan, listen up: This one is for you. The combination of sweet watermelon and briny cheese is one to delight all your guests. Not to mention, warm watermelon and cheese? It's certainly a conundrum for the senses.

6 **(6-inch) wooden skewers**

8 **to 10 ounces halloumi cheese, cut into 1-inch cubes**

4 **cups cubed seeded watermelon (1-inch cubes)**

¼ **cup chopped fresh mint**

Prepare a grill for direct-heat cooking and heat it to medium-high. Soak six 6-inch skewers in water for 15 to 20 minutes, then drain.

Skewer the halloumi and watermelon cubes in any pattern you like. (I like to make a variety of skewers, some with more watermelon, some with more cheese, so that guests can choose.)

Place the skewers directly over the heat and grill for about 3 minutes per side. The cheese will be lightly browned and warm inside. Remove the skewers from the grill and arrange them on a platter. Sprinkle the skewers with the mint and serve.

Asian Chicken Patties with Braised Bok Choy and Cabbage

Do you ever make something and it's so delicious, you think, "Is this real life? Did I just make these?" No? Just me? Well, you'll probably think that after you make this dish.

Paired with the braised greens, these patties are the perfect nutrient-dense, quick recipe that a busy weekday calls for. I intentionally made this recipe to yield a larger batch, because they reheat perfectly for leftovers (try them in the Asian Chicken Sweet Potato Burgers on page 208) or meal prepping.

SERVES 6

Dairy-Free
Gluten-Free
Grain-Free
Nut-Free
Paleo

- 2 **pounds ground chicken breast**
- 3 **teaspoons salt**
- 3 **garlic cloves, minced**
- 2 **green onions, light green and white parts only, thinly sliced**
- 1 **medium carrot, grated**
- 2 **tablespoons chopped fresh cilantro**
- 2 **tablespoons toasted sesame oil**
- ¼ **cup plus 1 tablespoon coconut aminos**
- 1 **teaspoon fish sauce**
- ½ **teaspoon ground ginger**
- 1½ **teaspoons coconut oil**
- 4 **baby bok choy, coarsely chopped**
- ½ **head green cabbage, shredded**
- 1½ **teaspoons unseasoned rice vinegar**

Put the ground chicken, 2½ teaspoons of the salt, the garlic, green onions, carrot, cilantro, sesame oil, 1 tablespoon of the coconut aminos, the fish sauce, and the ginger in a large bowl. Using your hands, combine the mixture well. Form the mixture into patties 3 to 4 inches in diameter, using about ⅓ cup for each. Set them aside on a cutting board or plate.

In a large skillet over medium heat, melt the coconut oil. When the oil is hot, working in batches, add the patties to the pan. Cook until the patties are lightly browned and their centers are no longer pink, 3 to 4 minutes on each side. Transfer the patties to a plate, loosely cover with aluminum foil, and set aside.

In the same pan, combine the remaining ¼ cup coconut aminos, the bok choy, cabbage, vinegar, and remaining ½ teaspoon salt and reduce the heat to medium-low. Toss the ingredients to combine them well. Cook, stirring, until the vegetables are soft, 10 to 11 minutes.

Serve the patties on top of the greens.

Greek Meatballs, Cukes, and Tzatziki

**SERVES
4 TO 6**

Gluten-Free

Grain-Free

Nut-Free

You know not every vegetable needs to be served hot and cooked, right? So many are delicious raw and cold, especially when paired with something heartier, like these herby meatballs.

TZATZIKI

- 2 cups plain whole-milk Greek yogurt
- ½ English cucumber, seeded and chopped
- 2 tablespoons chopped fresh dill
- ½ teaspoon lemon zest
- 1 tablespoon fresh lemon juice
- 1 teaspoon salt
- ¼ teaspoon freshly ground black pepper

CUCUMBERS

- 1½ English cucumbers, sliced
- ⅓ cup pitted kalamata olives, halved
- 1 teaspoon extra-virgin olive oil
- 1 teaspoon fresh lemon juice
- 2 teaspoons chopped fresh dill
- ¼ teaspoon salt

MEATBALLS

- 1½ pounds ground beef
- 2 teaspoons salt
- 3 garlic cloves, minced
- 2 tablespoons chopped fresh dill, plus more for serving (optional)
- 1 tablespoon chopped fresh mint
- 1 teaspoon lemon zest
- ½ teaspoon freshly ground black pepper
- 2 tablespoons coconut oil

To make the tzatziki: Combine the yogurt, cucumber, dill, lemon zest, lemon juice, salt, and pepper in a small bowl, cover, and refrigerate.

To make the cucumbers: Combine the cucumbers, olives, olive oil, lemon juice, dill, and salt in a medium bowl. Set aside.

To make the meatballs: Combine the ground beef, salt, garlic, dill, mint, lemon zest, and pepper in a large bowl. Using your hands, mix the ingredients just until

continues

**Greek Meatballs, Cukes,
and Tzatziki, continued**

incorporated (do not overmix). Roll the beef mixture into 1½-tablespoon balls and set them aside on a plate.

In a large skillet over medium heat, melt the coconut oil. When the oil is hot, add the meatballs, working in batches. Cook until the meatballs are browned, cooked through, and no longer pink in the middle, 6 to 8 minutes.

Plate the meatballs, tzatziki, and cucumbers on a platter. Garnish with additional dill, if desired, and serve family-style.

Chorizo-Stuffed Dates

MAKES
24 DATES

Gluten-Free
Grain-Free
Nut-Free
Paleo

This recipe is so perfect to make-and-take for any gathering. It requires minimal time and effort, and your friends and family will be thoroughly impressed.

24 **Medjool dates, pitted**

10 **ounces fresh (Mexican) chorizo, casings removed**

¼ **teaspoon red pepper flakes**

½ **cup apricot preserves**

¼ **cup crumbled queso fresco**

½ **lime**

Preheat the oven to 375°F.

Stuff each date with 1 to 2 teaspoons of the chorizo, depending on the size of the date. Place the stuffed dates on a baking sheet and bake for 15 minutes, until the chorizo has cooked through. Remove from the oven and let cool slightly.

Stir the red pepper flakes into the apricot preserves in a small bowl.

Arrange the dates on a platter. Top each date with 1 teaspoon of the apricot preserves and ½ teaspoon of the queso fresco. Squeeze a bit of lime juice over the top and serve.

Pan-Seared Salmon with Dill and Sautéed Spinach

SERVES 4

Gluten-Free

Grain-Free

Paleo

Recipes like this make me realize how easy it can be to stick to a healthy diet. It tastes delicious, leaves you satisfied, and fills your body with healthy nutrients. What more can you ask for?

1	**pound skin-on salmon fillet**
2¼	**teaspoons salt**
¼	**teaspoon lemon pepper**
2	**teaspoons extra-virgin olive oil, plus more if needed**
½	**onion, finely chopped**
4	**garlic cloves, minced**
1	**pound baby spinach**
⅓	**cup pine nuts, toasted (see Tip, page 20)**
1	**tablespoon chopped fresh dill**
4	**teaspoons crumbled feta cheese**

Season the salmon with 1½ teaspoons of the salt and the lemon pepper.

In a Dutch oven over medium-high heat, heat the olive oil. When the oil is hot, add the salmon, skin-side down, and cook, undisturbed, for 3 to 4 minutes. Flip the salmon and cook for 3 to 4 minutes more, until the salmon is cooked through and flakes easily with a fork. Transfer the salmon to a plate, cover it loosely with aluminum foil to keep warm, and set aside.

If the pan looks dry, add 1 teaspoon olive oil. Add the onion to the pan and cook over medium heat until softened and lightly browned, 6 to 7 minutes. Add the garlic and cook, stirring occasionally, for 1 minute.

Add the spinach and remaining ¾ teaspoon salt to the pan. Using tongs, toss the spinach frequently as it wilts down. Cook until all the spinach has wilted, 6 to 7 minutes.

To serve, divide the spinach among four serving plates. Place a portion of salmon on the spinach and top the salmon with the pine nuts, dill, and feta.

tip: I like using a Dutch oven for this recipe because it has high sides, which makes it easy to cook down a large amount of spinach without making a mess. If you don't have a Dutch oven, feel free to use any large pan or pot with high sides.

California Caprese

SERVES 4

Gluten-Free
Grain-Free
Nut-Free
Vegetarian

I'm pretty sure all you need to do to call something "California" around here is slap some avocado on it. Burgers, pizza, salads . . . add some avocado, and voilà! It's officially Californian. I changed up this caprese a little more than that, though, and added ingredients like goat cheese, arugula, and champagne vinegar to give it some extra layers of fresh flavor. It's downright delightful on a warm California day.

2 cups baby arugula

2 large heirloom tomatoes, sliced

2 avocados, sliced

1 tablespoon extra-virgin olive oil

2 teaspoons champagne vinegar

2 ounces soft goat cheese, crumbled (about ½ cup)

5 fresh basil leaves, chopped

Flaky sea salt and freshly ground black pepper

Place the arugula on a large platter and lay the tomato slices over the top. Arrange the avocado slices on top of the tomatoes and drizzle with the olive oil and vinegar. Sprinkle the goat cheese and basil over the salad. Season with flaky sea salt and pepper and serve.

Pesto Shrimp and Cauli Puree

Fresh pesto is a great way to take a meal to the next level with minimal effort, as evidenced by this recipe.

1 **pound raw medium shrimp, peeled and deveined**

2 **teaspoons salt**

1 **tablespoon extra-virgin olive oil**

2 **garlic cloves**

1 **head cauliflower (about 2 pounds), broken into florets**

1 **tablespoon butter or ghee (see Tip)**

½ **cup Vegan Pesto (page 20)**

Season the shrimp with 1 teaspoon of the salt. In a large skillet over medium heat, heat the olive oil. When the oil is hot, add the shrimp and cook until they are cooked through and light pink, 2 to 3 minutes on each side. Add the garlic, stir to combine, and cook for 1 minute. Remove the pan from the heat.

Fill a large pot with 2 to 3 inches of water and bring to a boil. Insert a steamer basket in the pot and add the cauliflower florets. Cover the pot and steam the cauliflower for 6 to 7 minutes, until tender. Transfer the cauliflower to a blender. Add the butter and the remaining 1 teaspoon salt, and blend on high speed until the cauliflower is a smooth puree.

To serve, divide the cauliflower puree among four serving plates. Top each portion with 2 tablespoons of the pesto and place one-quarter of the shrimp on the pesto.

tip: To make this dairy-free, substitute additional extra-virgin olive oil for the butter or ghee.

Burrata, Peach, and Blood Orange Salad

Want to know a secret? I sometimes get nervous when I cook for my friends and family. I feel that because of the nature of what I do, expectations are high when I have to create something special to serve them. So I tend to overthink things. "Should I make something healthy? Do they even *want* something healthy? What if they hate cilantro? What if my kiddos start arguing and I forget all about something on the stove and it gets ruined because I'm breaking up a fight over an L.O.L. doll? I should have a backup." Yeesh. After spending too much time trying to figure out what to bring to our friends Thuy and Morgan's house one night for dinner, I came up with this delightful dish. I figured that unless they didn't like burrata (and if they didn't like burrata, I would have to rethink our friendship), this would be a hit. And it was! So much so that I decided to add it to this book at the last minute. Next time you're trying to figure out what to bring to a friend's house for dinner, just remember this one.

SERVES 4

Gluten-Free
Grain-Free
Vegetarian

2 cups baby arugula

3 blood oranges (see Tip), peeled and sliced into discs

2 peaches, pitted and sliced

8 ounces burrata cheese

1½ teaspoons extra-virgin olive oil

1 teaspoon champagne vinegar

½ teaspoon flaky sea salt
 Microgreens, for garnish

Spread the arugula over a wide bowl or large platter and layer the oranges and peaches on top. Place the burrata in the center. Drizzle the olive oil and vinegar over the dish. Sprinkle with the flaky sea salt, garnish with microgreens, and serve.

tip: If you can't find blood oranges, regular ol' orange oranges will do just fine.

chapter 7

in an instant

HAS ANY OTHER COOKING INNOVATION of the last decade been as transformative for home cooks as the Instant Pot? Probably not.

When I was growing up, my grandmother had one of those clunky, *dangerous* pressure cookers of yore. I was taught to fear the pressure cooker and was suspicious of pressure-cooking anything for years.

Then along came the Instant Pot, the friendliest pressure cooker a girl could dream of. There was no worry, just delicious food that emerged transformed. Meats that took hours on the stovetop or in the oven were now done in a fraction of the time, tender and perfect. Soups became a breeze, and even rice came out better than ever.

The recipes in this chapter all utilize the magic of the Instant Pot. It's the number-one appliance I recommend to home cooks. I promise it won't be collecting dust, sitting next to that ice cream maker you just *had* to have.

179	Carnitas Más Rápido
180	Chicken Mole
185	Brad's Baby-Got-Back Ribs
186	Dairy-Free Rice Pudding
189	Chicken Tikka Masala Soup
191	Hawaiian Chicken Thighs
195	Short Rib Bolognese
196	Butternut Squash and Pancetta Risotto
199	Tomato and Red Pepper Soup

Carnitas Más Rápido

GREAT for LEFTOVERS

Fried bits of tender pork shoulder? Sign me up. I've always ordered carnitas at local taquerias, but once I realized how easy they can be to make at home, I started making them on a regular basis.

While there are many ways to make traditional carnitas, this is a briefer way that's convenient for busy home cooks. But guess what? It's just as delicious!

Use any leftovers in the Carnitas Ramen Noodles on page 203 or the Carnitas and Butternut Squash Tacos on page 207.

SERVES
8 TO 10

Dairy-Free

Gluten-Free

Grain-Free

Nut-Free

Paleo

1 **(5- to 6-pound) boneless pork shoulder, cut into quarters**

4 **tablespoons sea salt**

6 **garlic cloves, smashed**

2 **tablespoons cooking oil of your choice, such as avocado, coconut, or extra-virgin olive oil**

Put the pork shoulder, 3 tablespoons of the salt, and the garlic in the Instant Pot. Set it to the Meat/Stew function, lock the lid into place, and cook on high pressure for 120 minutes. Let the pressure release naturally.

Pull the pork out of the Instant Pot and transfer it to a large bowl. Drain the meat and discard the garlic and the liquid in the pot. Remove and discard any large portions of fat. Using a fork, break the meat into bite-size pieces. Add the remaining 1 tablespoon salt to the pork and gently stir to combine. At this point, if you're not serving the carnitas right away, store them as described in the Tip.

In a cast-iron skillet over medium-high heat, heat the oil. When the oil is hot, working in batches, add the carnitas and cook for 2 to 3 minutes on each side, until they have crisped. Use these carnitas for tacos or in breakfast frittatas, salads, or the following recipes in this book.

tip: *If you're planning to make these carnitas ahead of time to use throughout the week, cook them in the Instant Pot, let cool, then store them in an airtight container in the refrigerator for up to 5 days. Crisp them up in a skillet prior to using them.*

IN AN INSTANT

xo

Chicken Mole

I knew when I decided to tackle this recipe that it would be a tall order. Mole is a traditional Mexican sauce in which meat is simmered and stewed. It has a complex flavor, and it's either right or it's wrong. Making mole often requires a long, tedious process to get the flavors just right. But thanks to modern kitchen technology, we can make it in the comfort of our own homes with less labor, in a fraction of the time. You can serve this mole over Oven-Roasted Cauliflower Rice (page 73), with corn tortillas, over baked sweet potatoes, in enchiladas . . . the options are nearly endless!

**SERVES
4 TO 6**

*Dairy-Free
Gluten-Free*

3   pounds boneless, skinless chicken thighs

6½   teaspoons salt, plus more if needed

2   tablespoons sesame seeds

2   whole cloves

¼   teaspoon coriander seeds

¼   teaspoon aniseed

¼   cup avocado oil

5   dried pasilla chiles, stemmed and seeded

4   dried ancho chiles, stemmed and seeded

½   medium yellow onion, coarsely chopped

2   garlic cloves, smashed

¼   cup blanched raw almonds

¼   cup raisins

2   tablespoons pepitas (hulled pumpkin seeds)

1   tablespoon coconut sugar

½   teaspoon ground cinnamon

5   whole black peppercorns

2   corn tortillas, lightly charred and torn into pieces

1   canned chipotle chile in adobo sauce, seeded

2   ounces dark chocolate (see Tip), chopped

3   cups chicken broth

Chopped fresh cilantro, for garnish (optional)

Season the chicken thighs with 4 teaspoons of the salt and set aside.

Set the Instant Pot to the Sauté function on Normal. When the Instant Pot is hot, add the sesame seeds. Toast the sesame seeds, stirring frequently, until they are lightly browned, about 1 minute. Add the cloves, coriander, and aniseed. Toast the seeds and spices, stirring, until fragrant, about 1 minute. Remove the toasted seeds and spices from the Instant Pot and set aside.

continues

Chicken Mole, continued

Increase the Sauté setting to More and add the avocado oil to the pot. When the oil is hot, add the pasilla and ancho chiles. Fry them in the oil until they have softened a bit, 4 to 5 minutes. Remove the chiles from the Instant Pot and set them aside with the toasted seeds.

Add the onion to the hot oil and cook, stirring, until tender, 6 to 7 minutes. Add the garlic and cook for 1 minute more.

Return the toasted seeds and fried chiles to the Instant Pot. Add the almonds, raisins, pepitas, coconut sugar, cinnamon, peppercorns, tortillas, chipotle, chocolate, broth, 2 teaspoons salt, and the chicken thighs to the pot. Set the Instant Pot to Poultry on More, lock the lid into place, and cook for 60 minutes. Let the pressure release naturally.

Carefully remove the chicken and set aside. Working in batches, if necessary, carefully transfer the sauce from the Instant Pot to a blender and add the remaining ½ teaspoon salt. Blend on high speed until smooth. Taste and season with additional salt, if necessary. Return the sauce to the Instant Pot and set to Sauté. Simmer for 10 minutes, or until the sauce has thickened slightly. Return the chicken thighs to the Instant Pot and simmer for 5 minutes more to heat them through. Garnish with cilantro, if desired, and serve. Store any leftovers in an airtight container in the refrigerator for up to 5 days.

tip: *Find the darkest chocolate possible for this recipe. I used an 86% cacao chocolate bar for this recipe and loved the results. You can also substitute 1 tablespoon unsweetened cocoa powder for the chocolate.*

Brad's Baby-Got-Back Ribs

SERVES 4

Dairy-Free
Gluten-Free
Grain-Free
Nut-Free
Paleo

Brad has perfected the art of smoking and grilling ribs. We all love when he does it, but man, is it an all-day process! We are a demanding group of ladies over here, and sometimes when we want ribs, we want them ASAP. I challenged Brad to come up with an easy Instant Pot version that would rival those made during an all-day smoke-fest. And he did! Enjoy these smoky, tender, fall-off-the-bone ribs in just a fraction of the time.

3 tablespoons coconut sugar

2 teaspoons chili powder

2 teaspoons smoked paprika

2 teaspoons salt

1 teaspoon onion powder

1 teaspoon garlic powder

1 teaspoon freshly ground black pepper

½ teaspoon unsweetened cocoa powder

½ teaspoon cayenne pepper

1 (3- to 3½-pound) rack baby back ribs, cut into 2 slabs

3 tablespoons apple cider vinegar

¼ teaspoon liquid smoke

2 cups barbecue sauce (see Tip)

tip: There are a ton of clean barbecue sauces on the market today. Read labels and choose accordingly.

Combine the coconut sugar, chili powder, paprika, salt, onion powder, garlic powder, black pepper, cocoa powder, and cayenne in a small bowl. Generously coat the ribs with the rub, focusing on the meatier parts of the ribs.

Put the vinegar, liquid smoke, and 1 cup water in the Instant Pot. Insert a small steamer basket (I prefer a silicone one) into the Instant Pot. Nestle the rib sections vertically in the steamer basket. Set the Instant Pot to Meat/Stew, lock the lid into place, and cook on high pressure for 40 minutes.

While the ribs are cooking, preheat the oven to 450°F. Line a baking sheet with parchment paper.

When the ribs have cooked for 40 minutes, let the pressure release naturally.

Remove the ribs from the Instant Pot and place them on the parchment-lined baking sheet. Brush about 1 cup of the barbecue sauce over the ribs and bake them until warmed through, about 13 minutes.

Brush the remaining barbecue sauce over the ribs and serve.

Dairy-Free Rice Pudding

SERVES
4 TO 6

Dairy-Free

Gluten-Free

Nut-Free

Vegetarian

I've always loved rice pudding. I love how cozy it feels to curl up with a bowl and dig in. But these days, I don't love all the dairy in most rice puddings. Not only did I decide to remove the dairy in this version, but I also made things even easier by making it in the Instant Pot. God bless this machine, it does everything.

My kids love this recipe so much that they've been requesting it for breakfast. For added nutrients, I top it with some fresh berries.

1½ cups Arborio rice

Pinch of salt

2 large eggs

2½ cups full-fat coconut milk

½ cup pure maple syrup

1½ teaspoons pure vanilla extract

½ teaspoon ground cinnamon

½ cup raisins

Combine the rice, salt, and 1½ cups water in the Instant Pot. Set it to Manual, lock the lid into place, and cook for 4 minutes. Let the pressure release naturally.

Whisk together the eggs, coconut milk, maple syrup, vanilla, and cinnamon in a large bowl. Set the Instant Pot to the Sauté function and, while stirring continuously, slowly pour in the egg mixture. When the pudding starts to bubble, turn off the Instant Pot and stir in the raisins. Transfer the pudding to a glass container and let cool. It will thicken as it cools.

Cover and store in the refrigerator for up to 5 days.

tip: The rice pudding will continue to absorb liquid and thicken up as it cools and during storage. To make it creamy again, simply pour it into a skillet, add a bit of coconut milk, and reheat over medium-low heat. As you stir, add more coconut milk as needed to reach the desired consistency, until it is warmed through.

Chicken Tikka Masala Soup

GREAT for LEFTOVERS

SERVES
4 TO 6

Dairy-Free

Gluten-Free

Grain-Free

Nut-Free

Paleo

When I released my last book, a question I heard over and over was, "What's your favorite recipe in the book?" Well, friends, I am here to preemptively tell you that this may indeed be my favorite recipe in *this* book. At the very least, one of my favorites. This recipe epitomizes what eating well means to me: whole foods, convenience, and absolute freaking deliciousness. That's it. In my opinion, it doesn't need to be more complicated than that. I can guarantee that once you try this recipe, it will be in regular rotation in your home.

2 pounds boneless, skinless chicken thighs

4 teaspoons salt

2 teaspoons avocado oil

1 onion, chopped

3 garlic cloves, minced

3 cups chicken broth

5 whole black peppercorns

2 whole cloves

2 teaspoons coconut sugar

2 teaspoons grated fresh ginger (grated on a Microplane)

¼ teaspoon ground coriander

¼ teaspoon ground cardamom

¼ teaspoon cayenne pepper

¼ teaspoon ground nutmeg

¼ teaspoon ground cinnamon

¼ teaspoon ground cumin

1 (28-ounce) can crushed tomatoes

1 (13.5- to 14-ounce) can full-fat coconut milk

½ cup chopped fresh cilantro

Unsweetened shredded coconut, for garnish

Season the chicken thighs with 2 teaspoons of the salt and set aside.

Set the Instant Pot to the Sauté function and pour in the avocado oil. When the oil is hot, add the onion and cook until it is soft, 5 to 6 minutes. Add the garlic and cook, stirring so that the garlic doesn't burn, for 1 minute.

Add the chicken thighs, broth, peppercorns, cloves, coconut sugar, ginger, coriander, cardamom, cayenne, nutmeg, cinnamon, cumin, tomatoes, and remaining 2 teaspoons salt to the Instant Pot. Set the Instant Pot to Poultry, lock the lid into place, and cook on high pressure for 60 minutes. Let the pressure release naturally.

continues

IN AN INSTANT

xo

Chicken Tikka Masala Soup, continued

Remove the chicken from the Instant Pot and set aside to cool until you can touch it.

Use an immersion blender to blend the soup directly in the Instant Pot until it is smooth. Set the Instant Pot to the Sauté function and cook the soup for 10 minutes to thicken it. Using your hands, break the chicken into small pieces as you return it to the Instant Pot. Stir in the coconut milk.

To serve, pour the soup into bowls and top with cilantro and shredded coconut. Store leftovers in an airtight container in the refrigerator for up to 5 days.

Hawaiian Chicken Thighs

SERVES 4 TO 6

Dairy-Free

Gluten-Free

Grain-Free (option)

Nut-Free

Paleo (option)

I kid you not: The morning after I first made these delicious chicken thighs, I booked us a trip to Hawaii. Maybe that makes me unrelatable, but hear me out. We had originally been planning to take what I had dubbed "The Great All-American Southwest Road Trip" with the family: Vegas, Sedona, the Grand Canyon, and more! However, it was adding up to a lot of hours in the car and not a lot of hours vacationing. While I imagined us as the Brady Bunch on a road trip, Brad quipped it would be more like *National Lampoon*. When I sat down and took a bite of these tender thighs, my mind was instantly taken back to a previous Hawaiian vacation. The flavors reminded me of the state's peace and beauty, and the wonderful time we had there. When I sat down late that evening to plan what would have been a memorable but less than peaceful road trip . . . I realized I was longing for the peace. What I'm trying to get at is, don't blame me if you're suddenly transported to a tropical oasis in your mind after your first bite. It's delicious and, clearly, transformative.

2 pounds boneless, skinless chicken thighs

2½ teaspoons salt

¼ teaspoon freshly ground black pepper

½ cup plus 2 tablespoons coconut aminos

1 cup canned crushed pineapple, with its juice

1 tablespoon grated fresh ginger (grated on a Microplane)

1 tablespoon chili-garlic sauce

2 teaspoons toasted sesame oil

2 teaspoons unseasoned rice vinegar

½ cup unsweetened shredded coconut

1 red onion, chopped

Cooked white rice or Oven-Roasted Cauliflower Rice (page 73), for serving

6 slices fresh pineapple, for serving

3 green onions, light green and white parts only, sliced, for serving

⅓ cup chopped fresh cilantro, for serving

continues

Hawaiian Chicken Thighs, <u>continued</u>

Season the chicken thighs with the salt and pepper and set them aside.

Combine the coconut aminos, crushed pineapple with its juice, ginger, chili-garlic sauce, sesame oil, and vinegar in a medium bowl and stir until well combined. Set aside.

Set the Instant Pot to the Sauté function on Normal. When the pot is hot, add the shredded coconut. Toast the coconut, stirring frequently, until lightly browned, 1 to 2 minutes. Remove the coconut from the Instant Pot and set it aside.

Put the red onion and chicken thighs in the Instant Pot and pour the pineapple sauce over the top. Gently stir everything until the chicken is covered in the sauce. Set the Instant Pot to Manual, lock the lid into place, and cook on high pressure for 20 minutes. Let the pressure release naturally.

Transfer the chicken thighs to a plate and cover them loosely with aluminum foil to keep warm.

Set the Instant Pot to the Sauté function on Normal and cook the sauce for 5 to 6 minutes, until it has thickened a bit. Using an immersion blender, blend the sauce directly in the pot until it has a smooth, consistent texture.

To serve, place a serving of cooked white or cauliflower rice on each plate, place the chicken over the rice, and top with a slice of fresh pineapple. Spoon about ¼ cup of the sauce on top of each serving. Sprinkle the chicken generously with the green onions, toasted coconut, and cilantro.

Short Rib Bolognese

It's recipes like these that make the Instant Pot so popular. You can dump all the ingredients in and let 'er rip. Shortly thereafter, the food emerges as if you had been doting on it all day long. If only raising kids were this easy! Serve the Bolognese over zoodles, cauliflower rice (see page 73), mashed potatoes, sweet potatoes, roasted spaghetti squash, or gluten-free pasta. The possibilities are endless! Use any leftover Bolognese in the Creamy Mushroom Polenta with Short Rib Bolognese on page 212.

SERVES 8

Dairy-Free
Gluten-Free
Grain-Free
Nut-Free

3 pounds boneless beef short ribs

4½ teaspoons salt

1 (28-ounce) can crushed tomatoes

1 (15-ounce) can tomato sauce

1 cup red wine (use whatever you have on hand)

2 celery stalks, chopped

2 large carrots, chopped

½ large red onion, chopped

6 garlic cloves, minced

Season the short ribs all over with 3 teaspoons of the salt. Combine the crushed tomatoes, tomato sauce, wine, celery, carrots, onion, garlic, and remaining 1½ teaspoons salt in the Instant Pot. Nestle the short ribs into the sauce, making sure they are submerged. Set the Instant Pot to Meat/Stew, lock the lid into place, and cook on high pressure for 90 minutes. Let the pressure release naturally.

Press the Keep Warm/Cancel button and set the Instant Pot to the Sauté function. Cook the Bolognese, stirring occasionally and breaking the meat up into smaller pieces, for 10 minutes. The sauce will reduce and thicken. Skim any excess fat from the top. Serve over your favorite zoodle, pasta, or potatoes. Store any extra in the refrigerator in an airtight container for up to 5 days.

tip: *This is a great sauce to make a double batch of and freeze. It thaws quickly.*

Butternut Squash and Pancetta Risotto

I mean, if the Instant Pot doesn't make us feel like complete culinary cheaters, I don't know what does. Making delicious, creamy risotto in minutes? It sounds just too good to be true, but it's not.

I used to think of risotto as a main dish. While some people surely still do, I've come to think of it more as a side dish these days. That way, I can make sure the meal includes a healthy protein and lots of veggies. By moving risotto into the side dish category, I'm still able to enjoy it but in a smaller portion, alongside more nutrient-dense foods.

SERVES 6 TO 8

Gluten-Free

Nut-Free

2 tablespoons butter or ghee

1 yellow onion, chopped

2 teaspoons salt

¼ teaspoon freshly ground black pepper

6 ounces pancetta, diced

6 fresh sage leaves, minced

½ dry white wine

2 cups Arborio rice

2 cups cubed peeled butternut squash (about 10 ounces)

4 cups chicken broth

⅔ cup grated Parmesan cheese

½ cup whole milk

Set the Instant Pot to the Sauté function on High and add the butter. When the butter is hot, add the onion, 1 teaspoon of the salt, and the pepper and cook until the onion is soft, 5 to 6 minutes. Add the pancetta and cook until lightly browned, 4 to 5 minutes. Stir in the sage and cook until fragrant, about 1 minute. Add the wine and stir, scraping up any browned bits from the bottom of the Instant Pot. Add the rice and stir to combine. Cook, stirring occasionally, for about 2 minutes.

Add the squash and broth and stir to combine. Turn off the Sauté function, set the Instant Pot to Manual, lock the lid into place, and cook on high pressure for 6 minutes. Let the pressure release naturally.

Add the Parmesan, milk, and remaining 1 teaspoon salt to the risotto and stir until the risotto is creamy and the cheese has melted, 1 to 2 minutes. Serve hot.

Tomato and Red Pepper Soup

SERVES
4 TO 6

*Dairy-Free
(option)*

Gluten-Free

Grain-Free

Nut-Free

*Paleo
(option)*

The Instant Pot strikes again! Who knew you could whip up a delectable garden-fresh soup that tastes like it's been simmering away all day in no time? And it's delicious no matter what diet preference you follow.

1 tablespoon butter, ghee, or extra-virgin olive oil

1 medium onion, chopped

3 teaspoons salt

5 garlic cloves, minced

4 cups chicken broth

2 pounds tomatoes (6 or 7 medium), quartered

1 (6-ounce) jar fire-roasted red peppers, drained

2 teaspoons honey

1 teaspoon smoked paprika

½ teaspoon freshly ground black pepper

¼ cup chopped fresh basil, plus more for garnish if desired

⅓ cup half-and-half (optional; see Tip)

Set the Instant Pot to the Sauté function on High. Add the butter. When the butter is hot, add the onion and 1 teaspoon of the salt. Cook, stirring occasionally, until the onion is tender and lightly browned, 9 to 10 minutes. Add the garlic and cook, stirring frequently, for 1 minute. Add the broth, tomatoes, roasted peppers, honey, paprika, black pepper, and remaining 2 teaspoons salt.

Latch the lid onto the Instant Pot, select the Manual setting, and cook on high pressure for 12 minutes. Manually release the pressure.

Using an immersion blender, blend the soup directly in the Instant Pot until smooth. Add the basil and pulse the immersion blender a couple of times to incorporate it. Set the Instant Pot to the Sauté function and cook for 10 minutes to thicken the soup. If using the half-and-half, stir it in now.

Serve garnished with additional basil, if desired.

tip: To keep this dairy-free and Paleo, use extra-virgin olive oil instead of butter or ghee and omit the half-and-half.

chapter 8

leftovers again?

EITHER YOU LOVE LEFTOVERS or you don't. Personally, I do. Especially since I've become the head honcho of planning our meals around here.

Leftovers are a key component in maintaining a healthy, whole foods–based diet. It's unrealistic to think you are going to plan and cook every single meal from scratch, every single day. Leftovers give you the opportunity to make things a bit easier.

In this chapter, I repurpose leftovers from some of the other recipes in this book to make simple recipes even simpler.

203	Carnitas Ramen Noodles
204	Sweet Potato Nachos
207	Carnitas and Butternut Squash Tacos
208	Asian Chicken Sweet Potato Burgers
211	Chipotle Potato Pancake Stacks
212	Creamy Mushroom Polenta with Short Rib Bolognese
215	Chicken and Pesto–Stuffed Sweet Potatoes
216	Salmon and Pineapple Jicama Tacos
219	Cuban Sandwich on Tostones

Carnitas Ramen Noodles

This has quickly become one of my family's favorite recipes. The kids usually go for seconds. Okay, fine. Brad and I do as well. I have a feeling you will too.

SERVES 4 TO 6

Dairy-Free
Nut-Free

1 teaspoon avocado oil

1 medium yellow onion, chopped

2 teaspoons salt, plus more if needed

6 (3-ounce) packages ramen noodles

1 tablespoon toasted sesame oil

4 medium carrots, shredded (about 2 cups)

4 garlic cloves, minced

½ head cabbage, shredded (about 4 cups)

¼ cup coconut aminos

¼ cup tamari

2 to 3 cups leftover Carnitas Más Rápido (page 179), crisped (see Tip)

Bring a large pot of water to a boil.

In a large skillet over medium heat, heat the avocado oil. When the oil is hot, add the onion and 1 teaspoon of the salt and cook until the onion is tender and lightly browned, 7 to 8 minutes.

Add the ramen noodles to the boiling water and cook according to instructions. Drain and return to the pot. Add the sesame oil and gently toss to coat the noodles. Set aside to keep warm.

Add the carrots to the skillet with the onion and cook until softened, 4 to 5 minutes. Add the garlic and cook for 1 minute. Add the shredded cabbage and remaining 1 teaspoon salt and cook until the cabbage is tender, 3 to 4 minutes.

Add the vegetable mixture to the pot with the noodles. Add the coconut aminos, tamari, and carnitas. Toss the noodles, vegetables, and meat together until well combined. If necessary, season with salt. Refrigerate leftovers in an airtight container for up to 3 days.

tip: To crisp the carnitas, heat two teaspoons oil in a cast-iron skillet over medium-high heat. Season with two teaspoons salt and toss. Cook for two to three minutes on each side until they are perfectly crisped.

Sweet Potato Nachos

SERVES
2 TO 4

Gluten-Free

Grain-Free

Roasting up some sweet potato discs and topping them with leftovers can lead to some delicious meals. Top them with the proper ingredients, and you can even call them nachos.

2 medium sweet potatoes, peeled and sliced into ¼-inch-thick discs

2 teaspoons extra-virgin olive oil

½ teaspoon salt

1 to 2 cups chopped leftover cooked flank steak (see page 96)

1 cup leftover Tomato-Corn Salad (see page 000)

½ cup crumbled queso fresco

⅓ cup Cilantro-Jalapeño Aïoli (page 28)

¼ cup chopped fresh cilantro

1 avocado, diced

½ cup salsa of your choice, for serving

Preheat the oven to 425°F. Line a baking sheet with parchment paper; depending on the size of the sweet potato discs, you may need two baking sheets.

Toss the sweet potato discs, olive oil, and salt in a large bowl, then spread them over the parchment-lined sheet pan(s) in an even layer. Bake for 30 to 35 minutes, flipping the discs halfway through, until tender and golden brown on the edges.

Reheat the steak in a skillet or in the microwave.

Arrange the sweet potato discs on a platter. Top them with the flank steak, tomato-corn salad, queso fresco, aïoli, cilantro, avocado, and salsa. Serve.

Carnitas and Butternut Squash Tacos

SERVES
4 TO 6

Gluten-Free

Grain-Free
(option)

Nut-Free

This recipe came as a result of me simply cleaning out the fridge, which is fitting for this chapter. In fact, a lot of my recipe inspirations come from using up whatever tidbits I have that I don't want to go to waste! I love when I'm forced to use ingredients that I wouldn't traditionally think of together in a recipe and they make magic. I knew right away that this recipe deserved a place in this book. I have a feeling you'll agree!

1½ pounds butternut squash, peeled, seeded, and cubed

1 tablespoon plus 1 teaspoon extra-virgin olive oil

1¾ teaspoons salt

1 teaspoon smoked paprika

1 onion, thickly sliced

½ cup One-Minute Mayo (page 35)

½ teaspoon chipotle powder

1 garlic clove, minced

½ teaspoon fresh lime juice

2 cups coleslaw mix

2 cups leftover Carnitas Más Rápido (page 179), crisped (see page 203)

8 corn tortillas (see Tip), warmed

½ cup chopped fresh cilantro

4 ounces soft goat cheese, crumbled (about 1 cup)

½ to 1 cup salsa verde, for serving

Preheat the oven to 425°F. Line two baking sheets with parchment paper.

Combine the squash, 1 tablespoon of the olive oil, 1 teaspoon of the salt, and the paprika in a large bowl and toss to coat the squash thoroughly. Spread the squash on one of the parchment-lined baking sheets in an even layer. In the same bowl, combine the onion, remaining 1 teaspoon oil, and ½ teaspoon of the salt and toss or stir to coat the onion well. Spread the onion in an even layer on the second parchment-lined baking sheet. Bake the onion for 20 minutes and the squash for 30 to 35 minutes, stirring each about halfway through. Both the onion and the squash should be tender and lightly browned on the edges.

While the squash and onion are baking, stir together the mayonnaise, ground chipotle, garlic, lime juice, and remaining ¼ teaspoon salt in a small bowl.

To assemble the tacos, layer the coleslaw mix, carnitas, squash, and onion on the tortillas. Top with chipotle mayo, cilantro, goat cheese, and salsa verde and serve.

Asian Chicken Sweet Potato Burgers

MAKES 4
BURGERS

Dairy-Free

Gluten-Free

Grain-Free

Nut-Free

If you loved the Asian Chicken Patties in their original iteration, get ready to *really* love them now. With minimal effort, you can transform them into a totally different dish. While I love using roasted sweet potato slices as a "bun," you always have the option to use a regular bun. If you do opt to use the sweet potatoes, choose a sweet potato with a wide girth to give you the most surface area for your burger.

1	large sweet potato, sliced into ½-inch-thick discs
2	teaspoons extra-virgin olive oil
1½	teaspoons salt
⅛	teaspoon freshly ground black pepper
¼	cup One-Minute Mayo (page 35)
½	teaspoon fresh lime juice
½	teaspoon sriracha
¼	cup chopped fresh cilantro
2	tablespoons avocado oil
2	teaspoons coconut aminos
1	teaspoon toasted sesame oil
1	teaspoon unseasoned rice vinegar
2	cups coleslaw mix
4	leftover Asian Chicken Patties (page 161), warmed

Preheat the oven to 425°F. Line a baking sheet with parchment paper.

Combine the sweet potato discs, olive oil, 1 teaspoon of the salt, and the black pepper in a large bowl and toss to coat the sweet potato discs. Lay them in an even layer on the parchment-lined baking sheet and bake for 35 minutes, or until lightly browned and soft.

Combine the mayonnaise, lime juice, sriracha, and remaining ½ teaspoon salt in a small bowl and set aside.

Whisk together the cilantro, avocado oil, coconut aminos, sesame oil, and vinegar in a large bowl. Add the coleslaw mix and toss to coat well.

To assemble each burger, spread a sweet potato disc with sriracha mayonnaise and top with slaw and a chicken patty. Spread a bit of the sriracha mayo on a second sweet potato disc and top off the burger.

Chipotle Potato Pancake Stacks

This may be the ultimate weekend breakfast . . . using your weekday leftovers!

2 cups leftover Chipotle Smashed Potatoes (page 91)

¼ cup potato starch

9 large eggs

1 teaspoon salt

1 tablespoon plus 2 teaspoons avocado oil

4 cups baby spinach

½ cup salsa of your choice, for serving

In a large bowl, combine the potatoes, potato starch, 1 egg, and the salt and stir to combine well.

In a large skillet over medium heat, heat 1 tablespoon of the avocado oil. When the oil is hot, form the potato mixture into small patties, using ¼ cup for each, and add them to the oil. Fry the potato pancakes for 3 to 4 minutes on each side, until they are golden brown.

In a large nonstick skillet over medium heat, heat the remaining 2 teaspoons avocado oil. When the oil is hot, crack the remaining 8 eggs into the pan and fry for 1 to 2 minutes on each side, depending on how runny people like their yolks.

To serve, arrange 1 cup of the spinach on each plate and stack 2 potato pancakes on top. Top the potato pancakes with 2 fried eggs each and some salsa.

Creamy Mushroom Polenta with Short Rib Bolognese

SERVES 4

Gluten-Free
Nut-Free

If there were ever two recipes that needed to go together, it's this creamy polenta and saucy Short Rib Bolognese pairing. It's an Italian dream. They were meant to be besties.

2   **tablespoons extra-virgin olive oil**

1¼   **pounds cremini mushrooms, sliced**

3   **teaspoons salt**

3   **garlic cloves, minced**

1   **cup coarse cornmeal or corn grits**

2   **tablespoons butter or ghee**

½   **cup grated Parmesan cheese**

4   **cups leftover Short Rib Bolognese (page 195), warmed**

In a large skillet over medium heat, heat the olive oil. When the oil is hot, add the mushrooms and 1 teaspoon of the salt and stir to combine. Cook, stirring frequently, until the mushrooms are soft, 8 to 10 minutes. Add the garlic and cook for 1 minute. Remove from the heat.

Bring 4 cups water to a boil in a large saucepan. Add the cornmeal and the remaining 2 teaspoons salt and reduce the heat to maintain a simmer. Cook, whisking continuously, until the polenta starts to thicken and bubble, about 2 minutes, then cook, stirring occasionally, until the polenta is smooth and creamy, about 20 minutes more.

Stir the butter and Parmesan into the polenta. Fold in the cooked mushrooms.

Divide the polenta among four bowls and top each with 1 cup of the Bolognese. Serve immediately.

Chicken and Pesto–Stuffed Sweet Potatoes

SERVES 4

Gluten-Free
Grain-Free
Paleo

Have you ever had pesto and sweet potato together? Do you have any idea how well the garlic-y basil pairs against the sweet flesh of a sweet potato? Well, you're about to. This recipe is one you'll look at once and then be able to make on your own, over and over again. It's that simple and delicious.

2 **large sweet potatoes**

2 **teaspoons avocado oil**

1 **cup cherry tomatoes**

4 **tablespoons butter or ghee**

2 **teaspoons flaky sea salt**

2 **cups chopped leftover cooked chicken (see page 110) or rotisserie chicken**

1 **cup Vegan Pesto (page 20)**

Preheat the oven to 425°F. Line a baking sheet with aluminum foil.

Pierce the sweet potatoes several times with a fork and place them on the baking sheet. Bake for 45 to 50 minutes, until soft and tender.

While the sweet potatoes are baking, in a medium skillet over high heat, heat the avocado oil. When the oil is hot, add the cherry tomatoes and sear them on one side for 1 to 2 minutes. Gently shake the pan and sear the other side for 1 to 2 minutes. Set aside.

Remove the sweet potatoes from the oven and let cool slightly. When cool enough to handle, slice each sweet potato in half lengthwise and score crosshatches into the flesh. Add 1 tablespoon of the butter to each sweet potato half and sprinkle each with ½ teaspoon of the flaky sea salt.

Top each sweet potato half with ½ cup of the chicken and ¼ cup of the pesto. Divide the tomatoes evenly on top and serve.

Salmon and Pineapple Jicama Tacos

Tacos are the ultimate leftovers meal. I'm a firm believer that you can throw any leftovers into a tortilla and call it a taco, but I absolutely love the wild mix of flavors in this particular one. The sweetness of the pineapple alongside the heat of the sriracha is beautiful. In this recipe, I use jicama "tortillas," which are basically just thinly sliced discs of jicama. You can find them at some grocery stores, and I've included instructions for making them yourself in case they're not stocked at your store. But if that option doesn't excite you, traditional corn tortillas will work as well.

**MAKES
6 TACOS**

Dairy-Free

Gluten-Free

Grain-Free

¼ cup One-Minute Mayo (page 35)

1 teaspoon fresh lime juice

1 teaspoon honey

1 teaspoon sriracha

½ teaspoon toasted sesame oil

¼ teaspoon salt

2 cups shredded cabbage

4 tablespoons chopped fresh cilantro

6 jicama "tortillas" (see Tip)

1 to 1½ cups flaked leftover cooked salmon (see page 168; skin removed before flaking), warmed

6 (¼-inch-thick) fresh pineapple rings

¼ cup finely chopped red onion

¼ cup crushed roasted peanuts

Chili-garlic sauce, for serving

Stir together the mayonnaise, lime juice, honey, sriracha, sesame oil, and salt in a large bowl. Add the cabbage and 2 tablespoons of the cilantro and stir to coat the cabbage well.

To assemble each taco, lay a jicama tortilla flat and layer it with slaw, salmon, a pineapple ring, and red onion. Sprinkle the tacos with the peanuts and the remaining 2 tablespoons cilantro. Drizzle with chili-garlic sauce and serve.

tip: *To make jicama tortillas, peel a large jicama. Set a wide mandoline to cut slices about ⅛ inch thick and carefully slice the jicama into rounds. Set aside the 6 widest slices for the tacos and serve the rest alongside. Or snack on them while you cook!*

Cuban Sandwich on Tostones

MAKES 4
SANDWICHES

Gluten-Free

Grain-Free

Nut-Free

Paleo

Who says you need bread for a proper sandwich?

¼ cup One-Minute Mayo (page 35)

1 tablespoon tomato paste

1 tablespoon sweet pickle relish

4 medium-ripe slightly yellow plantains

2 tablespoons coconut oil

2 teaspoons salt

4 tablespoons brown mustard

4 slices Swiss cheese

2 cups leftover Carnitas Más Rápido (page 179), crisped (see page 203)

8 thin slices ham

8 sandwich-style pickle slices

½ cup sauerkraut, drained

Combine the mayonnaise, tomato paste, and relish in a small bowl and set aside.

Peel the plantains and cut each in half crosswise. In a large skillet over medium-high heat, melt the coconut oil. When the oil is hot, add the plantains and cook until they are lightly browned and tender, 2 to 3 minutes on each side. Use a slotted spatula to transfer the plantains to a sturdy cutting board. Press down on each plantain half with the flat bottom of a dish, until each is approximately ½ inch thick. Sprinkle the plantains with 1 teaspoon of the salt and return them to the pan. Cook over medium-high heat until the plantains are golden brown and crisped, 2 to 3 minutes per side. Transfer them to a paper towel–lined plate to drain. Sprinkle with the remaining 1 teaspoon salt.

To assemble each sandwich, spread 1 tablespoon of the mustard on a plantain slice and place it on a serving plate, mustard-side up. Top it with a slice of the Swiss cheese, ½ cup of the carnitas, 2 slices of ham, 2 pickle slices, and 2 tablespoons of the sauerkraut. Spread about 1 tablespoon of the mayo mixture on another plantain slice and close the sandwich, with the mayo side down. Repeat to assemble the remaining sandwiches, then serve. Don't forget the napkins!

LEFTOVERS AGAIN?

xo

chapter 9

weekend living

FOR ME, WEEKENDS are a time to unwind and enjoy the company of my friends and family. More often than not, that involves delicious food. While I pay closer attention to the healthy food choices I make during the week (and prefer them to be quick and easy), I'm more relaxed about my food choices when it comes to the weekend. I still want the foods I eat to be nourishing and wholesome. I just leave a little more wiggle room for decadence and preparation.

As the recipes in this chapter show, you can still indulge in delicious foods while keeping them whole and minimally processed.

222	**Chorizo and Potato Enchiladas**
226	**Sweet Potato Toast Panini**
229	**Apple-Cinnamon Scones**
231	**2 A.M. Tacos**
235	**Bob's Backyard Blender Salsa**
236	**The Best Damn Paleo Brownies**
239	**Bay Area Burgers**
242	**Cauliflower Gratin**
245	**Smoked Salmon Toasts with Crème Fraîche**
247	**Mexican Pizza**
249	**CBD Watermelon-Lime Spritz**
250	**Gluten-Free Blueberry Hand Pies**
254	**Peach-Bourbon Sipper**

Chorizo and Potato Enchiladas

SERVES
4 TO 6

Gluten-Free

*Grain-Free
(option)*

Nut-Free

Sometimes I still get scared at the thought of making my own [*fill in the blank*]. Enchilada sauce being one of those blanks. I always thought I would need a zillion impossible-to-source ingredients, a fancy cooking gadget, or some difficult technique to make it. I also figured it would take too much time. Not true! Homemade enchilada sauce is a breeze, and since I started making it, I'll never go back to store-bought. The hardest part—and it's not that hard—is finding the dried chiles. Most grocery stores stock them, but if they don't? Amazon does. Don't worry, I even checked for you. How's that for first-class cookbook service? Note that if you plan to use corn tortillas, it helps to heat the tortillas prior to stuffing them, as heat makes the tortillas more pliable and less likely to tear. Also note that different varieties and brands of tortillas will vary in size, so you may have extra filling left over. No worries! Simply stuff it into a bell pepper or serve it over a bed of spinach the next day for an easy and tasty lunch.

ENCHILADA SAUCE

- 1 teaspoon avocado oil
- ½ medium sweet onion, chopped
- 1½ teaspoons salt
- 2 garlic cloves, minced
- 3 dried ancho chiles, stemmed and seeded
- 2 dried guajillo chiles, stemmed and seeded
- 2 cups chicken broth
- 1 teaspoon smoked paprika
- ½ teaspoon ground chipotle chile
- ½ teaspoon unsweetened cocoa powder
- ½ teaspoon ground cumin

ENCHILADAS

- 2 medium russet potatoes, peeled and cubed
- 1 teaspoon salt
- 1½ teaspoons avocado oil
- 1 pound fresh (Mexican) chorizo, casings removed
- ½ medium sweet onion, diced
- 1¼ cups crumbled queso fresco
- 2 green onions, light green and white parts only, chopped
- ½ cup chopped fresh cilantro
- 10 corn tortillas or grain-free tortillas (see Tip), warmed

continues

Chorizo and Potato Enchiladas,
<u>continued</u>

To make the enchilada sauce: In a large pot over medium heat, heat the avocado oil. When the oil is hot, add the onion and ½ teaspoon of the salt. Cook, stirring, until the onion is tender, 7 to 8 minutes. Add the garlic and cook for 1 minute. Add the ancho chiles, guajillo chiles, broth, paprika, ground chipotle chile, cocoa powder, and cumin. Raise the heat to medium-high to bring everything to a low boil and cook for 5 to 6 minutes, until the chiles are softened.

Carefully transfer the contents of the pot to a blender and add the remaining 1 teaspoon salt. Blend on high speed for 10 seconds, or until the sauce is smooth.

Preheat the oven to 375°F.

To make the enchiladas: Put the potatoes in a large pot and add water just to cover them. Bring to a boil. Cook until the potatoes are fork-tender but still hold their shape, 10 to 15 minutes. Drain the potatoes and return them to the pot. Season the potatoes with the salt and set them aside.

In a large skillet over medium heat, heat 1 teaspoon of the avocado oil. When the oil is hot, add the chorizo and cook, gently breaking it apart with a wooden spoon as it cooks, until it is cooked through and lightly browned, 5 to 6 minutes. Use a slotted spoon to transfer the chorizo to the pot with the potatoes.

Pour the remaining ½ teaspoon avocado oil into the skillet. Add the sweet onion and cook over medium heat for 7 to 8 minutes, until the onion is soft and lightly browned. Add the sweet onion to the pot with the potatoes and chorizo. Add 1 cup of the queso fresco, the green onions, and ¼ cup of the cilantro. Stir lightly to combine everything.

Lay a tortilla on a plate, put about ½ cup of the filling in the middle, and roll it up. Place the enchilada seam-side down in a 9 by 13-inch glass baking dish. Repeat to fill the remaining tortillas, lining them up in the baking dish.

Pour the enchilada sauce over the rolled enchiladas, making sure to get sauce into every cranny and corner. Sprinkle the remaining ¼ cup queso fresco over the top. Bake the enchiladas for 25 to 30 minutes, until the sides are bubbling and the cheese has melted.

Sprinkle the remaining ¼ cup cilantro over the top and serve.

tip: When it comes to the type of tortilla to use, the choice is up to you. There are several grain-free varieties available at the grocery store that taste delicious, are pliable, and replicate the texture of traditional corn tortillas quite well.

Sweet Potato Toast Panini

MAKES 4
SANDWICHES

Gluten-Free

Grain-Free

Nut-Free

Panini that use toasted sweet potato slices rather than bread? Sign me up. This fun twist on traditional panini is a family favorite. Like any panini, it's best served right after you make it.

2 large sweet potatoes, peeled and sliced lengthwise into ¼-inch-thick slices

2 teaspoons butter or ghee, melted
Salt

4 teaspoons Dijon mustard

12 slices prosciutto

8 slices Havarti cheese

Toast the 8 largest sweet potato slices in a toaster or toaster oven until they are soft and lightly browned. (This will likely take several cycles of toasting.)

Heat a panini press or sandwich grill.

Brush a small amount of melted butter onto one side of each slice of toasted sweet potato and sprinkle with a small pinch of salt. Flip the slices over and spread with ½ teaspoon of the mustard. On four of the slices, layer a slice of prosciutto over the mustard, then a slice of Havarti, another slice of prosciutto, another slice of Havarti, and a final slice of prosciutto. Cover with the remaining sweet potato slices, mustard-side down. Place the sandwiches on the panini press, close the press, and grill for 3 to 4 minutes, until the cheese has melted.

Let the sandwiches cool for 2 minutes, then slice in half to serve.

tip: *Use a sweet potato with a wide girth to maximize the surface area for the "toast." If you prefer, you can bake the sweet potato slices in a preheated 425°F oven for 30 to 40 minutes.*

Apple-Cinnamon Scones

Scones are known for their flaky, lightly sweetened, crumbly goodness. While I've tried many grain-free versions, they never seem to replicate the unique texture that makes a scone a scone. Since scones aren't something we eat everyday anyhow, so they feel like a special treat, I decided to keep the grain in and opt for a gluten-free version. And what do you know? This gluten-free version replicates the flaky, delicate features of the original! I bet your friends and family won't even realize it's gluten-free.

**MAKES
6 SCONES**

Gluten-Free
Nut-Free
Vegetarian

½ **cup unsweetened applesauce**

½ **cup maple sugar
(see Tip)**

2 **large eggs**

1 **teaspoon pure vanilla extract**

2½ **cups gluten-free all-purpose flour, plus more for dusting**

1 **tablespoon baking powder**

1 **teaspoon ground cinnamon**

½ **teaspoon salt**

¼ **teaspoon ground cardamom**

8 **tablespoons salted butter, cut into cubes and chilled (see Tip)**

Combine the applesauce, maple sugar, eggs, and vanilla in a large bowl and whisk until well combined. In a separate bowl, mix together the flour, baking powder, cinnamon, salt, and cardamom.

Add the cold butter. Using a pastry cutter, cut the butter into the dry ingredients until evenly incorporated and broken down to about the size of peas; the dough will be crumbly. Slowly stir the butter-flour mixture into the applesauce mixture and combine well.

Cover the bowl and refrigerate the dough for 30 minutes.

While the dough is chilling, preheat the oven to 375°F. Line a baking sheet with parchment paper.

Lightly flour a work surface and turn the dough out onto it. Use your hands to form the dough into a flat disc 5 to 6 inches in diameter. Using a knife, cut the dough into 6 wedges. Use the knife to slightly separate the wedges from each other. Transfer the scones to the parchment-lined baking sheet. Bake for 25 to

continues

xo

Apple-Cinnamon Scones,
<u>continued</u>

30 minutes, until golden brown on top. Transfer the scones to a wire rack and let cool for 30 minutes prior to serving.

tips: You can find maple sugar in natural foods stores and online. It has a subtle flavor and works great in baking. If you'd like to substitute other sugars, you can use a mix of ¼ cup granulated sugar and ¼ cup packed light brown sugar for a similar flavor profile.

Before you start, cube the butter and put it back in the refrigerator. You want it to be as cold as possible when you incorporate it to ensure a flaky crust.

2 A.M. Tacos

MAKES
12 TACOS

Gluten-Free

Nut-Free

If you're in the know, you know exactly where the inspiration for these tacos came from. Some of the other names we threw around for them included 2 for 99¢ Tacos, Walk of Shame Tacos, and Late-Night Drunk College Tacos. Now you should *definitely* know where the inspiration came from. While we were making these, Brad questioned whether a fried taco should have a place in a healthy cookbook and I replied with a resounding *YES!* Because a) they're in the Weekend Living chapter, so game on; b) if you saw the ingredient list of the original tacos, you'd understand how much better these are for you; and c) I use grass-fed beef, organic non-GMO corn tortillas, and avocado oil, for crying out loud! I even found an organic American cheese.

So the next time you're craving a deep-fried taco late at night, remember you can easily make them at home with much better ingredients.

¼ cup plus 1 teaspoon avocado oil

1 pound ground beef

1 teaspoon salt

1 tablespoon chili powder

2 teaspoons onion granules

1 teaspoon garlic powder

½ teaspoon ground cumin

¼ teaspoon cayenne pepper

¾ cup refried beans

1 teaspoon fresh lime juice

6 slices American cheese, sliced in half diagonally

12 corn tortillas

1½ cups shredded iceberg lettuce

Hot sauce of your choice (see Tip)

In a large skillet over medium heat, heat 1 teaspoon of the avocado oil. When the oil is hot, add the ground beef, salt, chili powder, onion granules, garlic powder, cumin, and cayenne. Cook, using a spatula to break up the ground beef as it cooks, until the beef is cooked through and lightly browned, 7 to 8 minutes. Add the refried beans and lime juice and stir to combine.

Transfer the beef mixture to a blender and blend for 10 to 20 seconds, until it is a uniform consistency—what I like to call "meat paste."

To assemble each taco, lay a triangle of American cheese on one half of a tortilla. Spread 2 tablespoons of the meat filling over the top of the cheese, being careful not to spread the meat all the way to the edge.

continues

xo

2 A.M. Tacos, continued

Repeat with the remaining tortillas, cheese, and meat filling.

Line a plate with a few layers of paper towels and place it near the stovetop.

Pour the remaining ¼ cup avocado oil into a small skillet and heat over medium-high heat. When the oil is hot, place a tortilla flat in the pan and let it sit for 15 to 20 seconds, until the tortilla becomes pliable. Fold the empty side of the tortilla over the top to create the "taco shape." Cook the taco for 10 seconds more, then flip it and cook the other side for 20 to 30 seconds, until the shell has crisped up and is lightly browned. Immediately transfer the taco to the paper towel–lined plate to drain. Gently open the taco and fill it with 2 tablespoons of the shredded lettuce and hot sauce to taste. Repeat with the remaining tacos. Serve hot.

tip: *You can use any sort of hot sauce for this recipe, but I find a red pepper hot sauce most closely resembles the flavor of my taco muse. My personal favorite for this recipe is the jalapeño pepper hot sauce from Trader Joe's. It's really clean and has a bold yet not overly spicy flavor.*

Bob's Backyard Blender Salsa

When I was growing up, my dad, Bob, always planted a summer garden that was loaded with tomatoes and peppers. We had so many tomatoes each year that my dad started making giant vats of salsa to use them up. Imagine the largest bowl you have in your kitchen and double that. That's how big these batches of salsa ended up being. I hesitate to tell you that it was eaten up in about a week . . . but it was. We put it on everything, and God only knows how many bags of tortilla chips we went through. Because you probably won't mow through five gallons of salsa the way we did, I reduced the size of the original batch. My dad and I developed the official recipe for you. Don't be afraid to tinker with it and make it your own. If you love cilantro, add some more! Need it to be a bit spicier? Leave in some of the jalapeño seeds and ribs. The beauty of this recipe lies in its flexibility.

**MAKES
8 CUPS**

Dairy-Free
Gluten-Free
Grain-Free
Nut-Free
Paleo
Vegan
Vegetarian

3 **pounds tomatoes, quartered**

1 **small to medium white onion, chopped**

1½ **cups chopped fresh cilantro**

2 **medium jalapeños, seeds and ribs removed, chopped**

1 **tomatillo, husked, rinsed, and quartered**

3 **garlic cloves, chopped**

2 **tablespoons salt**

tip: This salsa works with a wide variety of tomatoes, although I find beefsteak to be the best choice.

Combine half the tomatoes, one-quarter of the onion, ½ cup of the cilantro, half the jalapeños, half the tomatillo, half the garlic, and 1 tablespoon of the salt in a blender. Run the blender on high speed for 10 to 20 seconds, until the mixture is completely pureed and has a liquid, smoothie-like texture. Pour it into a large bowl.

Combine the remaining tomatoes, another quarter of the onion, ½ cup of the cilantro, and the remaining jalapeño, tomatillo, and garlic in the blender and pulse several times until everything is finely chopped. Add this to the puree in the bowl.

Add the remaining onion, ½ cup cilantro, and 1 tablespoon salt to the bowl and stir to combine. Cover the bowl or transfer the salsa to an airtight container and store in the refrigerator for up to 7 days.

Serve with chips, over eggs, or with the Salmon and Pineapple Jicama Tacos on page 216.

The Best Damn Paleo Brownies

This one time, on Instagram . . . My friend and I were going to a Dead & Company show (she's a Grateful Dead fan and I'm a John Mayer fan), so she tagged me in one of John Mayer's Instagram posts promoting the upcoming show. I responded cheekily, letting her know I'd be bringing some Paleo brownies to indulge in, because Grateful Dead . . . San Francisco Bay Area . . . *you know* ☺. And Barbra Streisand, of all people, liked my comment. Like, the *real* Barbra Streisand. Not only did she like my comment, she asked for the recipe! So Babs, here's the recipe, just for you. Enjoy your Paleo brownies! As far as chocolate chips go, my favorite ones are from Enjoy Life. They're free of all common allergens such as dairy, nuts, and soy, and make for delicious baking.

MAKES 9 BROWNIES

Gluten-Free

Grain-Free

Paleo

Vegetarian

¼ **cup plus 1 teaspoon coconut oil**

2 **large eggs**

1 **large egg white**

¾ **cup coconut sugar**

¼ **cup pure maple syrup**

1 **teaspoon pure vanilla extract**

⅓ **cup almond flour**

¼ **cup unsweetened cocoa powder**

2 **teaspoons coconut flour**

1 **teaspoon tapioca flour**

1 **teaspoon espresso powder**

¼ **teaspoon baking soda**

¼ **teaspoon salt**

4 **tablespoons butter or ghee**

1 **(6.5-ounce) bag semisweet chocolate chips (1 cup)**

Preheat the oven to 350°F. Grease an 11-inch square glass baking dish with 1 teaspoon of the coconut oil.

In the bowl of a stand mixer fitted with the whisk attachment, combine the eggs, egg white, and coconut sugar and beat on medium-high speed until the eggs start to foam lightly, about 2 minutes. Add the maple syrup and vanilla and beat for 1 minute more.

In a separate bowl, combine the almond flour, cocoa powder, coconut flour, tapioca flour, espresso powder, baking soda, and salt. Using a spatula, gently fold the dry ingredients into the whipped egg mixture until well incorporated.

In a medium saucepan, combine the butter, remaining ¼ cup coconut oil, and 5 ounces (about ¾ cup) of the chocolate chips. Heat over medium heat, stirring

continues

The Best Damn Paleo Brownies, continued

frequently, until the chocolate has melted and the mixture is well combined. Let the chocolate cool slightly. Fold the melted chocolate into the batter. Gently fold in the remaining chocolate chips.

Pour the batter into the prepared pan and smooth the top. Bake for 30 to 35 minutes, until a toothpick inserted into the center comes out clean. Let the brownies cool in the pan to room temperature.

Cut the brownies into 9 squares. Store in an airtight container at room temperature for up to 5 days.

Bay Area Burgers

As a California native who has spent the majority of her life in the San Francisco Bay Area, it's safe to say my heart is firmly locked in. For better or worse. For worse, because it can take you an hour and a half to drive twenty miles, a one-thousand-square-foot fixer-upper can run you about a million, and I don't speak tech. For better, because it's a mecca for creativity and innovation, the weather is just right, and its geography gives us easy access to beautiful beaches and mountains. Not to mention that MC Hammer and E-40 have dominated our playlists at one point or another and the Bay Area is one of the best places in the world to live if you're a foodie. Truly.

This burger is simply a hat tip to my home. Thank you, Bay Area, for keeping it real, smart, bizarre, crunk, delicious, and everything in between.

**MAKES
4 BURGERS**

*Gluten-Free
(option)*

Nut-Free

GARLIC AÏOLI

- ⅓ cup One-Minute Mayo (page 35)
- 4 garlic cloves, minced
- ⅛ teaspoon salt
- Freshly cracked black pepper

BURGERS

- 1 pound ground beef
- 1¾ teaspoons salt
- ¼ teaspoon freshly ground black pepper
- 2 slices bacon
- ½ pound cremini mushrooms, sliced
- 4 ounces Brie cheese, sliced
- 4 hamburger buns (see Tips), toasted
- 2 cups micro sprouts
- 1 cup sauerkraut, drained

To make the garlic aïoli: Combine the mayonnaise, garlic, and salt in a small bowl. Season with pepper. Cover and refrigerate.

To make the burgers: Put the ground beef, 1½ teaspoons of the salt, and the pepper in a bowl and use your hands to combine everything gently but thoroughly. Form the beef mixture into 4 patties and set aside on a large plate.

Heat a large skillet over medium heat. When the pan is hot, add the bacon and cook until crisp, 7 to 9 minutes, flipping it once halfway through the cooking time. Remove the bacon from the pan and lay it on a paper towel–lined plate to drain.

Add the mushrooms and the remaining ¼ teaspoon salt to the fat in the pan. Cook the mushrooms over medium heat, stirring frequently, until tender, 6 to 7 minutes. Remove the mushrooms from the pan and set them aside.

continues

Increase the heat under the pan to medium-high. Add the beef patties and cook until browned on the bottom, 3 to 4 minutes. Flip the patties and cook for 2 minutes. Top the patties with the Brie and cook until the cheese begins to melt, 1 to 2 minutes more. The burgers will be medium-well at this point.

To assemble each burger, spread some of the garlic aïoli on the cut sides of a bun. Place ½ cup of the sprouts on the bottom bun. Top with one-quarter of the sautéed mushrooms. Place a burger patty on top of the mushrooms. Top the burger with ¼ cup of the sauerkraut and ½ slice bacon and cover it with the other half of the bun.

Grab a napkin and take a giant bite while you hum "Tell Me When to Go" by our pal E-40.

tips: Don't handle the ground beef too much when mixing the ingredients or forming the patties, as that will render the meat a bit tougher. Be gentle when you're forming the patties, and you'll have a juicier, more tender burger.

To make this gluten-free, just use gluten-free buns.

Cauliflower Gratin

I'm not going to say this dish is necessarily healthy. (But it has vegetables!) Rather, I will say that it's an indulgent whole-food recipe that isn't meant for every day. Weekends and holidays are the perfect spot for this one. Our family makes it every Thanksgiving. Although I'm pretty sure you'll want to eat it every day.

**SERVES
4 TO 6**

Gluten-Free
Grain-Free
Nut-Free

1 head cauliflower (about 2 pounds), broken into small florets

1 tablespoon extra-virgin olive oil

2 teaspoons salt

5 slices bacon, chopped

2 tablespoons butter

2 tablespoons gluten-free all-purpose flour

1¼ cups whole milk

¼ teaspoon freshly ground black pepper

½ cup grated Asiago cheese

⅓ cup grated Gruyère cheese

1 teaspoon chopped fresh thyme

½ cup crushed pork rinds (chicharrónes)

Preheat the oven to 425°F. Line a baking sheet with parchment paper.

Put the cauliflower, olive oil, and 1 teaspoon of the salt in a large bowl and toss to coat. Spread the cauliflower on the parchment-lined baking sheet and bake for 25 to 30 minutes, until the cauliflower is tender and golden brown on the edges.

Meanwhile, put the bacon in a saucepan over medium heat and cook until lightly crisped, about 7 minutes. Remove the bacon with a slotted spoon and lay it on a paper towel–lined plate to drain. Discard the bacon grease from the saucepan (not down the drain!), but don't wash out the pan.

Return the saucepan to medium heat. When it's hot, add the butter and let it melt. While whisking continuously, slowly sprinkle the flour over the butter and whisk until incorporated, then slowly add the milk and whisk until the sauce is smooth. Add the remaining 1 teaspoon

continues

Cauliflower Gratin, continued

salt, the pepper, the Asiago, and the Gruyère and whisk until the cheeses have melted and the sauce is smooth. Turn off the heat.

When the cauliflower is done roasting, transfer it to a large bowl and pour the cheese sauce over it. Add the thyme and bacon and stir until the cauliflower is completely coated. Pour everything into an 8-inch square glass baking dish and top with the crushed pork rinds. Reduce the oven temperature to 375°F and bake for 20 to 25 minutes, until the gratin starts to bubble. Let cool for 5 to 10 minutes prior to serving.

Smoked Salmon Toasts with Crème Fraîche

Sometimes weekend breakfasts call for a longer, more meaningful morning in the kitchen. And sometimes you just want a quick breakfast that feels special without all the hassle.

While this breakfast may feel like a delight, the reality is, it's a simple recipe that takes only a few minutes to pull together. Whip it up and grab your ~~paper~~ phone to peruse leisurely while you sip your coffee.

1   teaspoon extra-virgin olive oil

4   large eggs, beaten

⅛   teaspoon salt

4   slices bread (see Tips), toasted

4   ounces smoked salmon

4   teaspoons crème fraîche (see Tips)

1   teaspoon chopped fresh dill

In a medium pan over medium heat, heat the olive oil. When the oil is hot, pour in the eggs and sprinkle with the salt. Gently stir the eggs and fold the curds over each other, scrambling the eggs and cooking them until most of the liquid is gone.

To serve, divide the toast slices among four plates. Top each slice with one-quarter of the scrambled eggs. Place one-quarter of the smoked salmon over the eggs. Top the salmon with 1 teaspoon of the crème fraîche and sprinkle with ¼ teaspoon of the dill. Serve immediately.

tips: Use a gluten-free bread to make this gluten-free. I know—duh, right? My personal favorite is from Canyon Bakehouse.

Feel free to swap out the crème fraîche for cream cheese. Spread it on the toast first, then top with the scrambled eggs and salmon.

Mexican Pizza

When I was in my twenties, my roommate, Ami, and I used to order a pizza very similar to this one more often than I should ever admit. The pizza place that served up all our late-night desires has since closed, so I decided to keep its legend alive through this recipe. Feel free to make your own pizza crust if you want to, but in the spirit of this book, I prefer to buy one. There are so many gluten-free pizza crust options available on the market these days. You can find anything from grain-free versions to broccoli or cauliflower crusts.

SERVES
2 TO 4

Gluten-Free
Nut-Free

1 **(9- to 10-inch) gluten-free pizza crust of your choice**

½ **teaspoon extra-virgin olive oil**

⅓ **pound fresh (Mexican) chorizo, casings removed**

½ **cup refried pinto or black beans**

¼ **cup freshly diced tomatoes**

½ **teaspoon salt**

½ **teaspoon garlic powder**

¾ **cup shredded medium cheddar cheese**

¼ **cup canned sliced jalapeños, drained**

⅓ **cup cherry tomatoes, halved**

¼ **cup chopped fresh cilantro**

Hot sauce of your choice, for serving

Preheat the oven to 425°F. Prepare the pizza crust according to the manufacturer's instructions.

In a medium skillet over medium heat, heat the olive oil. When the oil is hot, add the chorizo and cook, using a wooden spoon to gently break it up, until it is cooked through and lightly browned, 5 to 6 minutes. Set aside.

Combine the refried beans, diced tomatoes, salt, and garlic powder in a bowl. Evenly spread the mixture over the pizza crust. Top with the chorizo and then the cheddar. Sprinkle the jalapeños and cherry tomatoes over the top.

Bake the pizza for 15 minutes, or until the crust is cooked through, the toppings are hot, and the cheese has melted. Remove the pizza from the oven and sprinkle the cilantro over the top.

To serve, cut the pizza into 8 slices and drizzle with hot sauce.

CBD Watermelon-Lime Spritz

SERVES 1

Dairy-Free

Gluten-Free

Grain-Free

Nut-Free

Vegan

Vegetarian

I've been making this recipe for a few years now, but it wasn't until recently that I started adding CBD to it. Of late we've been hearing all about the benefits of CBD, and it only made sense to add it to a cool, refreshing drink. The amount of CBD you use will depend on the concentration and your preferences. Add the amount that is recommended by the manufacturer and that you are comfortable with. If you're hesitant about CBD for whatever reason, you can leave it out and the drink will be just as delicious.

8 to 12 fresh mint leaves

1 ounce fresh lime juice

Ice cubes

12 ounces (1½ cups) watermelon kombucha (I like GT's)

1½ ounces gin

1 serving CBD isolate powder or oil (optional)

2 ounces lime-flavored sparkling water

Mint sprig and watermelon or lime slice, for garnish

Muddle the mint leaves and lime juice together in the bottom of a large glass (such as a pint glass) and add some ice. Add the kombucha, gin, and CBD (if using) and stir gently. Top off with the sparkling water. Stir gently to combine everything.

Serve garnished with a mint sprig and a small slice of watermelon.

Gluten-Free Blueberry Hand Pies

I joke with two of my friends (who are both also named Michelle) that when I retire, I want to open up a hand pie shack amid the wineries in our hometown. It will be fun and funky, with picnic tables, and we'll play Jay-Z and be known for the best hand pies around. Sounds amazing, right? I'm trying to convince the other Michelles that they'll want in on this brilliant idea because then we can name it Michelles' Hand Pie Shack. (Grammar snobs everywhere will appreciate that one.) They haven't yet agreed, but maybe after this recipe, they will.

**MAKES
6 PIES**

Gluten-Free

Vegetarian

2½	cups fresh blueberries
¼	cup plus 2 teaspoons honey
1½	teaspoons fresh lemon juice
¼	teaspoon pure almond extract
⅛	teaspoon ground cinnamon
	Salt
2½	cups gluten-free all-purpose flour, plus more for dusting
2	tablespoons coconut sugar
12	tablespoons butter, cut into cubes and chilled
2	large eggs
2	tablespoons ice water

Combine the blueberries, ¼ cup of the honey, the lemon juice, almond extract, cinnamon, a pinch of salt, and ¼ cup water in a saucepan. Cook over medium-high heat, stirring occasionally, for 3 to 4 minutes. Reduce the heat to medium and simmer, stirring frequently, until the blueberries have broken down, 15 minutes more. The filling should be thick and will continue to thicken as it cools. Transfer the filling to an airtight container and refrigerate until it's fully cool.

Put the flour, coconut sugar, and 1 teaspoon salt in a large bowl and combine. Using a pastry cutter, cut the butter into the flour until a crumbly dough starts to form. Beat 1 of the eggs and add it to the dough along with the ice water. Using your hands, gently fold the dough together, smoothing out any pieces of butter between your fingers. Work the dough into a ball that holds together, then divide it into 4 portions. Gently flatten each portion into a disc and wrap in plastic wrap. Refrigerate the dough for at least 1 hour.

continues

Preheat the oven to 400°F. Line a baking sheet with parchment paper.

Working with one portion of the dough at a time, on a well-floured surface, gently roll out the dough to ⅛ inch thick. If the dough starts to stick, flour the surface and rolling pin again. Using a pizza cutter, cut the dough into 3 by 4-inch rectangles. Repeat with the remaining dough; you will need 12 rectangles.

Arrange 6 of the dough rectangles on the parchment-lined baking sheet and place 2 tablespoons of the blueberry filling in the center each. Use a knife to create two small slits in the center of the remaining rectangles. Place these over the filling and crimp together the edges by gently pressing a fork along the perimeter of each hand pie.

Whisk together the remaining egg, 1 teaspoon water, and the remaining 2 teaspoons honey. Lightly brush this egg wash over the tops of the hand pies. Bake the pies for 25 to 30 minutes, until they are golden brown. Transfer the pies to a wire rack to cool before serving.

Serve warm or at room temperature. Store any leftovers in an airtight container at room temperature for up to 4 days.

tip: *Not all gluten-free flours are created equal. They can't just remove the gluten from wheat flour; it doesn't work like that. Gluten-free flours are made with a combination of several non-wheat flours. Because different brands vary so much in the amounts and types of flours they use, there will be some variation in the crust here depending on what brand you use. I tested these pies with several different flours, and my favorite was Cup-4-Cup, as it best mimicked wheat flour.*

WEEKEND LIVING

Peach-Bourbon Sipper

MAKES
ABOUT
½ CUP SYRUP
AND
2 COCKTAILS

Dairy-Free

Gluten-Free

Nut-Free

Vegetarian

I love me a good cocktail. Like, looooove me one. Personally, I don't like cocktails that are too alcohol-forward or too sweet. I like easy-drinkin' drinks, and this one is oh so easy to drink.

This cocktail tastes best on a warm summer evening, sitting on your front porch or in your backyard, but if that isn't an option, staring out your window at the street below on a blustery, gray day works, too!

HONEY-CINNAMON SYRUP

- ¼ **cup honey**
- ¼ **teaspoon ground cinnamon**

FOR THE COCKTAILS

- 3 **ounces peach juice or peach puree**
- 2 **ounces bourbon**
- 1 **ounce fresh lemon juice**
  Ice cubes
  Peach slices, for garnish

To make the syrup: Combine the honey, cinnamon, and ¼ cup water in a saucepan over medium heat. Bring to a simmer, stirring occasionally, until the honey has dissolved. Let cool. Store in an airtight container at room temperature or in the refrigerator for up to 2 weeks (the recipe makes enough syrup for about 8 cocktails).

To make the cocktails: Combine the peach juice, bourbon, lemon juice, ½ ounce of the Honey-Cinnamon Syrup, and ice cubes in a cocktail shaker. Shake vigorously for 20 seconds. And shake it again, this time getting your booty into it. Strain the cocktail into two coupe glasses and serve. If you don't have coupe glasses, any ol' glass—a red Solo cup, or that leftover paper cup from your kid's last birthday party—will do! Garnish with a peach slice.

ACKNOWLEDGMENTS

First and foremost, I need to thank Brad, Camryn, and Teagan. You are all so supportive of me and the work I do, and I am forever appreciative. Not only do you embrace me as a wife and mother, but you allow me room to make space for my dreams. I cherish you all.

Mom and Dad, your continued support and excitement bring me so much gratitude and joy. Thank you for stepping in to play "mom" all the days I was busy in the kitchen.

To my editor, Justin Schwartz, thank you for seeing this project through and lighting the way for it to happen. I'm always grateful for your expertise and knowledge.

To my publishing team at HMH, thank you for your fantastic efforts in bringing this book to fruition.

To my agent, Lisa Grubka, I'm so grateful for your support in creating this book as I envisioned it to be. Thank you.

Betsy Haley, my dream food stylist, thank you for all the creativity and beauty you have brought to this book. I'm so thankful to have had our paths cross and to be able to create together. Many thanks to Jessie Bloom for assisting Betsy.

To Jennifer and Lindsay Skog, thank you for all your hard work on the beautiful photos in this book and for making me feel like a rock star.

And to Kristen Boehmer, my sister from another mister. I can't imagine any of this without your constant support, love, and friendship. I could write pages about how much I adore you, but that would be an entirely separate book. *Mahalo nui loa.*

Last but not least, thank you to each and every one of you who have purchased my books, follow me on social media, and make my recipes. Your excitement for what I do fuels and amplifies my mission of bringing whole foods back into our households. My deepest gratitude to you all—I see each and every one of you.

RECIPE	Dairy-Free	Gluten-Free	Grain-Free	Nut-Free	Paleo	Vegan	Vegetarian
Sweet Potato and Sage Zoodle Sauce, page 14	×	×	×	×	×	×	×
Chai Spice Blend, page 16	×	×	×	×	×	×	×
Honey-Curry Dip, page 19	×	×	×	×	×		×
Vegan Pesto, page 20	×	×	×		×	×	×
Creamy Romesco Sauce, page 23	×	×	×		×		×
Zesty Dill-Kefir Dressing, page 24		×	×	×			×
Chocolate Coco Whip, page 27	×	×	×	×	×	×	×
Cilantro-Jalapeño Aïoli, page 28	×	×	×	×	×		×
Strawberry-Feta Vinaigrette, page 31		×	×	×			×
Dairy-Free Cinnamon Maple Cashew Coffee Creamer, page 32	×	×	×		×	×	×
One-Minute Mayo, page 35	×	×	×	×	×		×
Banana Bread Overnight Oats, page 39	×	×				×	×
Breakfast Sausage Meatballs, page 40	×	×	×	×	×		
Apple-Cinnamon Mini Frittatas, page 43	×	×	×	×	×		×
Arugula Melon Prosciutto Bowls, page 45	×	×	×	×	×		
Orange-Ginger Smoothie Packs, page 46	×	×	×	×	×	×	×
Hearty Mediterranean Salad with Lemon-Dill Dressing, page 49		×	×	×			×
Sweet Potato Hash Egg Cups, page 50	×	×	×	×	×		
Ground Beef Trifle with Cauliflower Puree, page 53		×	×	×	×		
Hangry Man Plate, page 55		×	×	×			
Buffalo Chicken Frittata, page 58		×	×	×	×		
Spaghetti Squash Pizza, page 63		×	×	×			
Grain-Free Everything Bagel Crackers, page 64	×	×	×		×		×
Sriracha Salmon and Broccoli, page 67	×	×	×	×	×		
Sheet Pan Eggplant Parmesan, page 69		×	×	×			×
Oven-Roasted Cauliflower Rice, page 73	×	×	×	×	×	×	×

RECIPE	Dairy-Free	Gluten-Free	Grain-Free	Nut-Free	Paleo	Vegan	Vegetarian
Spatchcocked Chimichurri Chicken and Carrot Fries, page 74	×	×	×	×	×		
Sausages with Mustard Parsnips and Onions, page 77	×	×	×	×	×		
Sheet Pan "Fried" Chicken and BBQ Kale Chips, page 79	×	×	×		×		
Sheet Pan Beef Jerky, page 83	×	×	×	×	×		
Sheet Pan Harissa Chicken and Veggies, page 84	×	×	×	×	×		
Balsamic Chicken Thighs with Mushrooms and Caramelized Onions, page 89	×	×	×	×	×		
Chipotle Smashed Potatoes, page 91		×	×	×			
Plantain "French Toast" Dippers, page 92	×	×	×	×	×	×	×
Shrimp and Shishitos, page 95	×	×	×	×	×		
Grilled Flank Steak with Tomato-Corn Salad, page 96	×	×		×			
Pork and Maple Butternut Squash, page 98	×	×	×	×	×		
Matcha-Kale Smoothie, page 101	×	×	×	×	×	×	×
Apple "Pasta," page 103	×	×	×		×	×	×
Strawberry-Balsamic Beef Medallions, page 104		×	×	×			
Dairy-Free Cold-Brew Latte, page 106	×	×	×		×	×	×
Firecracker Cauliflower, page 109	×	×	×		×	×	×
Pan-Roasted Chicken and Crispy Shaved Brussels Sprouts, page 110	×	×	×	×	×		
Chile-Lime Plantains, page 113	×	×	×	×	×	×	×
Caramelized Cherries and Yogurt, page 114		×	×	×			×
Chai-Spiced Kettle-Style Apples, page 119		×	×	×	×	×	×
Ranchero Skillet Breakfast Tacos, page 120		×	×	×			
Summer Corn Chowder, page 123		×	×	×	×		
Black Bean Soup, page 126	×	×	×	×		×	×
Salmon Curry, page 129	×	×	×	×	×		

RECIPE	Dairy-Free	Gluten-Free	Grain-Free	Nut-Free	Paleo	Vegan	Vegetarian
Grain-Free Crispy Honey Shrimp and Bok Choy, page 131	×	×	×	×	×		
Sun-Dried Tomato and Goat Cheese Frittata, page 135		×	×	×			
Cauliflower Rice Paella, page 136	×	×	×	×			
Artichoke and Kalamata Cod, page 139	×	×	×	×	×		
Beverly's Chicken Adobo, page 141	×	×	×	×	×		
Garam Masala Rice and Apricots, page 143	×					×	×
Grain-Free Fish Sticks and Tartar Sauce, page 147	×	×	×		×		
Seared Ahi and Cabbage, page 149	×	×	×	×			
Drive-Through Burger Bowls, page 153	×	×	×	×	×		
Italian Sub Skewers, page 154		×	×	×			
Harissa-Spiced Cauliflower Fritters, page 157	×	×	×				×
Halloumi and Watermelon Skewers, page 158		×	×	×			×
Asian Chicken Patties with Braised Bok Choy and Cabbage, page 161	×	×	×	×	×		
Greek Meatballs, Cukes, and Tzatziki, page 162		×	×	×			
Chorizo-Stuffed Dates, page 167		×	×	×	×		
Pan-Seared Salmon with Dill and Sautéed Spinach, page 168		×	×		×		
California Caprese, page 171		×	×	×			×
Pesto Shrimp and Cauli Puree, page 172	×	×	×		×		
Burrata, Peach, and Blood Orange Salad, page 175		×	×				×
Carnitas Más Rápido, page 179	×	×	×	×	×		
Chicken Mole, page 180	×	×					
Brad's Baby-Got-Back Ribs, page 185	×	×	×	×	×		
Dairy-Free Rice Pudding, page 186	×	×		×			×
Chicken Tikka Masala Soup, page 189	×	×	×	×	×		
Hawaiian Chicken Thighs, page 191	×	×	×	×	×		
Short Rib Bolognese, page 195	×	×	×	×			
Butternut Squash and Pancetta Risotto, page 196		×		×			
Tomato and Red Pepper Soup, page 199	×	×	×	×	×		
Carnitas Ramen Noodles, page 203	×			×			
Sweet Potato Nachos, page 204		×	×				
Carnitas and Butternut Squash Tacos, page 207		×	×	×			
Asian Chicken Sweet Potato Burgers, page 208	×	×	×	×			
Chipotle Potato Pancake Stacks, page 211		×					
Creamy Mushroom Polenta with Short Rib Bolognese, page 212		×		×			
Chicken and Pesto–Stuffed Sweet Potatoes, page 215		×	×		×		
Salmon and Pineapple Jicama Tacos, page 216	×	×	×				
Cuban Sandwich on Tostones, page 219		×	×	×			
Chorizo and Potato Enchiladas, page 222		×	×	×			
Sweet Potato Toast Panini, page 226		×	×	×			
Apple-Cinnamon Scones, page 229		×		×			×
2 A.M. Tacos, page 231		×		×			
Bob's Backyard Blender Salsa, page 235	×	×	×	×	×	×	×
The Best Damn Paleo Brownies, page 236		×	×		×		×
Bay Area Burgers, page 239		×		×			
Cauliflower Gratin, page 242		×	×	×			
Smoked Salmon Toasts with Crème Fraîche, page 245		×		×			
Mexican Pizza, page 247		×		×			
CBD Watermelon-Lime Spritz, page 249	×	×	×	×		×	×
Gluten-Free Blueberry Hand Pies, page 250		×					×
Peach-Bourbon Sipper, page 254	×	×		×			×

INDEX

Note: Page references in *italics* indicate photographs.

Ahi, Seared, and Cabbage,
    149–50, *151*
Aïoli
    Cilantro-Jalapeño, 28, *29*
    Garlic, 239, *240*
Almonds
    Creamy Romesco Sauce, *22*, 23
    Garam Masala Rice and Apricots,
        143
Apple(s)
    Chai-Spiced Kettle-Style, *118*, 119
    -Cinnamon Mini Frittatas, *42*, 43
    -Cinnamon Scones, *228*, 229–30
    "Pasta," *102*, 103
Apricots and Rice, Garam Masala, 143
Artichoke and Kalamata Cod, 139
Arugula
    Burrata, Peach, and Blood
        Orange Salad, *174*, 175
    California Caprese, *170*, 171
    Hearty Mediterranean Salad with
        Lemon-Dill Dressing, *48*, 49
    Melon Prosciutto Bowls, 44, *45*
Avocados
    California Caprese, *170*, 171
    mashing, 11
    ripening, 10
    Sweet Potato Nachos, 204, *205*

Bacon
    Bay Area Burgers, 239–41, *240*
    Butternut Squash and Pancetta
        Risotto, 196, *197*
    Cauliflower Gratin, 242–44, *243*
    Sweet Potato Hash Egg Cups,
        50, *51*
Balsamic Chicken Thighs with
    Mushrooms and Caramelized
    Onions, *88*, 89–90
Banana(s)
    Bread Overnight Oats, *38*, 39
    Matcha-Kale Smoothie, 101
    Orange-Ginger Smoothie Packs,
        46, 47

Basil
    California Caprese, *170*, 171
    Vegan Pesto, 20, *21*
Bean(s)
    Black, Soup, 126, *127*
    Hearty Mediterranean Salad with
        Lemon-Dill Dressing, *48*, 49
    Mexican Pizza, *246*, 247
    Salmon Curry, *128*, 129–30
    Sheet Pan Harissa Chicken and
        Veggies, 84, *85*
    2 A.M. Tacos, 231–32, *233*
Beef
    Bay Area Burgers, 239–41, *240*
    Creamy Mushroom Polenta with
        Short Rib Bolognese, 212, *213*
    Drive-Through Burger Bowls,
        152, 153
    Greek Meatballs, Cukes, and
        Tzatziki, 162–64, *163*
    Grilled Flank Steak with Tomato-
        Corn Salad, 96, *97*
    Ground, Trifle with Cauliflower
        Puree, 52, 53–54
    Jerky, Sheet Pan, *82*, 83
    Medallions, Strawberry-Balsamic,
        104–5, *105*
    Ranchero Skillet Breakfast Tacos,
        120, *121*
    Short Rib Bolognese, *194*, 195
    Sweet Potato Nachos, 204, *205*
    2 A.M. Tacos, 231–32, *233*
Blueberry Hand Pies, Gluten-Free,
    250–53, *251*
Bok Choy
    and Cabbage, Braised, Asian
        Chicken Patties with, *160*, 161
    and Grain-Free Crispy Honey
        Shrimp, 131–32, *133*
Bolognese, Short Rib, *194*, 195
Bourbon
    Caramelized Cherries and
        Yogurt, 114, *115*
    -Peach Sipper, 254, *255*

Broccoli and Sriracha Salmon, 67
Brownies, The Best Damn Paleo,
    236–38, *237*
Brussels Sprouts
    Crispy Shaved, and Pan-Roasted
        Chicken, 110, *111*
    shredding quickly, 11
Buffalo Chicken Frittata, 58, *59*
Burger Bowls, Drive-Through, *152*, 153
Burgers
    Asian Chicken Sweet Potato,
        208, *209*
    Bay Area, 239–41, *240*

Cabbage
    and Bok Choy, Braised, Asian
        Chicken Patties with, *160*, 161
    Carnitas Ramen Noodles,
        202, 203
    and Seared Ahi, 149–50, *151*
Carnitas
    and Butternut Squash Tacos, *206*,
        207
    Más Rápido, *178*, 179
    Ramen Noodles, *202*, 203
Carrot(s)
    Carnitas Ramen Noodles, *202*, 203
    Fries and Spatchcocked
        Chimichurri Chicken, 74–76,
        75
    Orange-Ginger Smoothie Packs,
        46, 47
    Salmon Curry, *128*, 129–30
Cashew(s)
    Maple Cinnamon Coffee Creamer,
        Dairy-Free, 32, *33*
    Vegan Pesto, 20, *21*
Cauliflower
    breaking into florets, 11
    Firecracker, *108*, 109
    Fritters, Harissa-Spiced, *156*, 157
    Gratin, 242–44, *243*
    Pesto Shrimp and Cauli Puree,
        172, *173*

Puree, Ground Beef Trifle with, *52*, 53–54

Rice, Oven-Roasted, *72, 73*

Rice Paella, 136–38, *137*

Sheet Pan Harissa Chicken and Veggies, *84, 85*

CBD Watermelon-Lime Spritzer, *248, 249*

Chai Spice Blend, 16, *17*

Chai-Spiced Kettle-Style Apples, *118, 119*

Cheese

    Bay Area Burgers, 239–41, *240*

    Buffalo Chicken Frittata, 58, *59*

    Burrata, Peach, and Blood Orange Salad, *174, 175*

    California Caprese, *170, 171*

    Carnitas and Butternut Squash Tacos, *206, 207*

    Cauliflower Gratin, 242–44, *243*

    Chorizo and Potato Enchiladas, 222–25, *223*

    Cuban Sandwich on Tostones, *218, 219*

    Goat, and Sun-Dried Tomato Frittata, *134*, 135

    Halloumi and Watermelon Skewers, 158, *159*

    Italian Sub Skewers, 154, *155*

    Mexican Pizza, *246, 247*

    rinds, adding to soup, 11

    Sheet Pan Eggplant Parmesan, *68*, 69–70

    Spaghetti Squash Pizza, *62, 63*

    Strawberry-Balsamic Beef Medallions, 104–5, *105*

    Strawberry-Feta Vinaigrette, *30*, 31

    Sweet Potato Toast Panini, 226, *227*

    2 A.M. Tacos, 231–32, *233*

Cherries

    Caramelized, and Yogurt, 114, *115*

    pitting, 9

Chicken

    Adobo, Beverly's, *140*, 141–42

    Buffalo, Frittata, 58, *59*

    Cauliflower Rice Paella, 136–38, *137*

    Mole, 180–82, *181*

Pan-Roasted, and Crispy Shaved Brussels Sprouts, 110, *111*

Patties, Asian, with Braised Bok Choy and Cabbage, *160, 161*

and Pesto–Stuffed Sweet Potatoes, *214*, 215

Sausages with Mustard Parsnips and Onions, 77

Sheet Pan "Fried," and BBQ Kale Chips, *78*, 79–80

shredding, tip for, 9

Spatchcocked Chimichurri, and Carrot Fries, 74–76, *75*

Sweet Potato Burgers, Asian, 208, *209*

Thighs, Balsamic, with Mushrooms and Caramelized Onions, *88*, 89–90

Thighs, Hawaiian, 191–92, *193*

Tikka Masala Soup, *188*, 189–90

and Veggies, Sheet Pan Harissa, 84, *85*

Chiles

    Bob's Backyard Blender Salsa, *234*, 235

    Chicken Mole, 180–82, *181*

    Chipotle Smashed Potatoes, 91

    Chorizo and Potato Enchiladas, 222–25, *223*

    Cilantro-Jalapeño Aïoli, 28, *29*

Chimichurri Spatchcocked Chicken and Carrot Fries, 74–76, *75*

Chocolate

    The Best Damn Paleo Brownies, 236–38, *237*

    Chicken Mole, 180–82, *181*

    Coco Whip, *26, 27*

Chowder, Summer Corn, *122*, 123–24

Cilantro

    Bob's Backyard Blender Salsa, *234*, 235

    -Jalapeño Aïoli, 28, *29*

    Spatchcocked Chimichurri Chicken and Carrot Fries, 74–76, *75*

Cinnamon

    -Apple Mini Frittatas, *42, 43*

    -Apple Scones, *228*, 229–30

    Chai Spice Blend, 16, *17*

Maple Cashew Coffee Creamer, Dairy-Free, 32, *33*

Coconut

    Chocolate Coco Whip, *26, 27*

    Hawaiian Chicken Thighs, 191–92, *193*

Cod

    Artichoke and Kalamata, 139

    Grain-Free Fish Sticks and Tartar Sauce, *146*, 147–48

Coffee

    Creamer, Dairy-Free Cinnamon Maple Cashew, 32, *33*

    Dairy-Free Cold-Brew Latte, 106, *107*

Corn

    Chowder, Summer, *122*, 123–24

    Sweet Potato Nachos, 204, *205*

    -Tomato Salad, Grilled Flank Steak with, *96*, 97

Crackers, Grain-Free Everything Bagel, 64–66, *65*

Cucumbers

    Greek Meatballs, Cukes, and Tzatziki, 162–64, *163*

    Hearty Mediterranean Salad with Lemon-Dill Dressing, *48*, 49

Curry, Salmon, *128*, 129–30

Curry-Honey Dip, 18, 19

Dates, Chorizo-Stuffed, *166*, 167

Desserts

    Apple "Pasta," *102*, 103

    The Best Damn Paleo Brownies, 236–38, *237*

    Caramelized Cherries and Yogurt, 114, *115*

    Chai-Spiced Kettle-Style Apples, *118, 119*

    Dairy-Free Rice Pudding, 186, *187*

    Gluten-Free Blueberry Hand Pies, 250–53, *251*

Dill

    -Kefir Dressing, Zesty, 24, *25*

    -Lemon Dressing, Hearty Mediterranean Salad with, *48*, 49

    and Sautéed Spinach, Pan-Seared Salmon with, 168, *169*

xo

Dips. *See also* Mayo
  Honey-Curry, *18*, 19
Drinks
  CBD Watermelon-Lime Spritzer, *248*, 249
  creating foamy lattes, 10–11
  Dairy-Free Cold-Brew Latte, 106, *107*
  Matcha-Kale Smoothie, 101
  Orange-Ginger Smoothie Packs, 46, *47*
  Peach-Bourbon Sipper, 254, *255*

Eggplant Parmesan, Sheet Pan, *68*, 69–70
Egg(s)
  Apple-Cinnamon Mini Frittatas, *42*, 43
  Buffalo Chicken Frittata, 58, *59*
  Cups, Sweet Potato Hash, 50, *51*
  fried, adding to meals, 10
  Ranchero Skillet Breakfast Tacos, 120, *121*
  retrieving broken shells, 10
  Smoked Salmon Toasts with Crème Fraîche, 245
  spilled, cleaning tip, 10
  Sun-Dried Tomato and Goat Cheese Frittata, *134*, 135
Enchiladas, Chorizo and Potato, 222–25, *223*
Everything Bagel Crackers, Grain-Free, 64–66, *65*

Fish
  Artichoke and Kalamata Cod, 139
  deboning, 10
  Pan-Seared Salmon with Dill and Sautéed Spinach, 168, *169*
  Salmon and Pineapple Jicama Tacos, 216, *217*
  Salmon Curry, *128*, 129–30
  salting before cooking, 10
  Seared Ahi and Cabbage, 149–50, *151*
  Smoked Salmon Toasts with Crème Fraîche, 245
  Sriracha Salmon and Broccoli, 67
  Sticks, Grain-Free, and Tartar Sauce, *146*, 147–48

Frittatas
  Apple-Cinnamon Mini, *42*, 43
  Buffalo Chicken, 58, *59*
  Sun-Dried Tomato and Goat Cheese, *134*, 135
Fritters, Harissa-Spiced Cauliflower, *156*, 157
Fruit. *See also* specific fruits
  freezing, 10

Garam Masala Rice and Apricots, 143
Garlic Aïoli, 239, *240*
Ginger
  Chai Spice Blend, 16, *17*
  -Orange Smoothie Packs, 46, *47*
  storing, 11
Grains. *See* Oats; Rice
Grease splatters, 9
Greens. *See* Arugula; Kale; Lettuce; Spinach

Ham. *See also* Prosciutto
  Cuban Sandwich on Tostones, *218*, 219
Hand Pies, Gluten-Free Blueberry, 250–53, *251*
Harissa
  Chicken and Veggies, Sheet Pan, 84, *85*
  -Spiced Cauliflower Fritters, *156*, 157
Herbs. *See* Basil; Cilantro; Sage
Honey
  -Curry Dip, *18*, 19
  measuring, 10

Italian Sub Skewers, 154, *155*

Jerky, Beef, Sheet Pan, *82*, 83
Jicama Tacos, Salmon and Pineapple, 216, *217*

Kale
  Chips, BBQ, and Sheet Pan "Fried" Chicken, *78*, 79–80
  -Matcha Smoothie, 101
Kefir-Dill Dressing, Zesty, 24, *25*
Kitchen hacks, tips, and tricks, 9–11
Kitchen shears, 11

Lattes
  Dairy-Free Cold-Brew, 106, *107*
  foamy, tip for, 10–11
Lemon-Dill Dressing, Hearty Mediterranean Salad with, *48*, 49
Lettuce
  Drive-Through Burger Bowls, *152*, 153
  2 A.M. Tacos, 231–32, *233*

Maple
  Cinnamon Cashew Coffee Creamer, Dairy-Free, 32, *33*
  and Pork Butternut Squash, 98–100, *99*
Matcha-Kale Smoothie, 101
Mayo
  Cilantro-Jalapeño Aïoli, 28, *29*
  Garlic Aïoli, 239, *240*
  One-Minute, 34, *34*
  Sriracha, 149–50, *151*
Meat. *See also* Beef; Pork
  raw, slicing thinly, 10
  salting before cooking, 10
  thawing, 9
Meatballs
  Breakfast Sausage, 40, *41*
  forming, tip for, 11
  Greek, Cukes, and Tzatziki, 162–64, *163*
Melon
  Arugula Prosciutto Bowls, 44, 45
  CBD Watermelon-Lime Spritzer, *248*, 249
  Halloumi and Watermelon Skewers, 158, *159*
Mole, Chicken, 180–82, *181*
Mushroom(s)
  Bay Area Burgers, 239–41, *240*
  and Caramelized Onions, Balsamic Chicken Thighs with, *88*, 89–90
  Grain-Free Crispy Honey Shrimp and Bok Choy, 131–32, *133*
  Hangry Man Plate, 55–56, *57*
  Polenta, Creamy, with Short Rib Bolognese, 212, *213*

Nachos, Sweet Potato, 204, *205*
Noodles, Carnitas Ramen, *202*, 203
Nuts. *See* Almonds; Cashew(s); Pine nuts

Oats, Banana Bread Overnight, *38*, 39
Olives
    Artichoke and Kalamata Cod, 139
    Hearty Mediterranean Salad with Lemon-Dill Dressing, *48*, 49
    Italian Sub Skewers, 154, *155*
    Sheet Pan Harissa Chicken and Veggies, 84, *85*
    Spaghetti Squash Pizza, *62*, 63
Onions
    Caramelized, and Mushrooms, Balsamic Chicken Thighs with, *88*, 89–90
    and Parsnips, Mustard, Sausages with, 77
    quick-pickling, 11
Orange
    Blood, Burrata, and Peach Salad, *174*, 175
    -Ginger Smoothie Packs, 46, *47*

Paella, Cauliflower Rice, 136–38, *137*
Pancake Stacks, Chipotle Chicken, *210*, 211
Pancetta and Butternut Squash Risotto, 196, *197*
Parchment paper, working with, 11
Parsnips and Onions, Mustard, Sausages with, 77
"Pasta," Apple, *102*, 103
Patties, Asian Chicken, with Braised Bok Choy and Cabbage, *160*, 161
Peach
    -Bourbon Sipper, 254, *255*
    Burrata, and Blood Orange Salad, *174*, 175
Pepper(s). *See also* Chiles
    Black Bean Soup, 126, *127*
    Creamy Romesco Sauce, *22*, 23
    Hearty Mediterranean Salad with Lemon-Dill Dressing, *48*, 49
    Italian Sub Skewers, 154, *155*
    Red, and Tomato Soup, *198*, 199

Salmon Curry, *128*, 129–30
Shrimp and Shishitos, *94*, 95
Spaghetti Squash Pizza, *62*, 63
Summer Corn Chowder, *122*, 123–24
Pesto
    and Chicken–Stuffed Sweet Potatoes, *214*, 215
    Shrimp and Cauli Puree, *172*, *173*
    Vegan, 20, *21*
Pineapple
    Hawaiian Chicken Thighs, 191–92, *193*
    Orange-Ginger Smoothie Packs, 46, *47*
    and Salmon Jicama Tacos, 216, *217*
Pine nuts
    Pan-Seared Salmon with Dill and Sautéed Spinach, 168, *169*
    Vegan Pesto, 20, *21*
Pizza
    Mexican, *246*, 247
    Spaghetti Squash, *62*, 63
Plantain(s)
    Chile-Lime, *112*, 113
    Cuban Sandwich on Tostones, *218*, 219
    "French Toast" Dippers, *92*, *93*
Polenta, Creamy Mushroom, with Short Rib Bolognese, 212, *213*
Pork. *See also* Bacon; Sausage(s)
    Brad's Baby-Got-Back Ribs, *184*, 185
    Carnitas and Butternut Squash Tacos, *206*, 207
    Carnitas Más Rápido, *178*, 179
    Carnitas Ramen Noodles, *202*, 203
    Cuban Sandwich on Tostones, *218*, 219
    and Maple Butternut Squash, 98–100, *99*
Potato(es). *See also* Sweet Potato(es)
    Beverly's Chicken Adobo, *140*, 141–42
    Buffalo Chicken Frittata, 58, *59*
    Chipotle, Pancake Stacks, *210*, 211
    Chipotle Smashed, 91
    and Chorizo Enchiladas, 222–25, *223*
    Hangry Man Plate, 55–56, *57*

Poultry. *See* Chicken; Turkey
Prosciutto
    Arugula Melon Bowls, 44, *45*
    Italian Sub Skewers, 154, *155*
    Sweet Potato Toast Panini, 226, *227*
Pudding, Dairy-Free Rice, 186, *187*

Ramen Noodles, Carnitas, *202*, 203
Ranchero Skillet Breakfast Tacos, 120, *121*
Rice
    and Apricots, Garam Masala, 143
    Beverly's Chicken Adobo, *140*, 141–42
    Butternut Squash and Pancetta Risotto, 196, *197*
    leftover, reheating, 11
    Pudding, Dairy-Free, 186, *187*
Risotto, Butternut Squash and Pancetta, 196, *197*
Romesco Sauce, Creamy, *22*, 23

Sage and Sweet Potato Zoodle Sauce, *14*, 15
Salad dressings
    Strawberry-Feta Vinaigrette, *30*, 31
    Zesty Dill-Kefir, 24, *25*
Salads
    Burrata, Peach, and Blood Orange, *174*, 175
    California Caprese, *170*, 171
    Hearty Mediterranean, with Lemon-Dill Dressing, *48*, 49
Salmon
    Curry, *128*, 129–30
    Pan-Seared, with Dill and Sautéed Spinach, 168, *169*
    and Pineapple Jicama Tacos, 216, *217*
    Smoked, Toasts with Crème Fraîche, 245
    Sriracha, and Broccoli, 67
Salsa, Bob's Backyard Blender, *234*, 235
Sandwiches
    Cuban, on Tostones, *218*, 219
    Sweet Potato Toast Panini, 226, *227*

xo

Sauces. *See also* Mayo
  Bob's Backyard Blender Salsa, *234*, 235
  Creamy Romesco, *22*, 23
  Short Rib Bolognese, *194*, 195
  Sweet Potato and Sage Zoodle, 14, *15*
  Tartar, *146*, 147
  Tzatziki, 162, *163*
  Vegan Pesto, 20, *21*
Sauerkraut
  Bay Area Burgers, 239–41, *240*
  Cuban Sandwich on Tostones, *218*, 219
  Sausages with Mustard Parsnips and Onions, 77
Sausage(s)
  Breakfast, Meatballs, 40, *41*
  Cauliflower Rice Paella, 136–38, *137*
  Chipotle Smashed Potatoes, 91
  Chorizo and Potato Enchiladas, 222–25, *223*
  Chorizo-Stuffed Dates, *166*, 167
  Italian Sub Skewers, 154, *155*
  Mexican Pizza, *246*, 247
  with Mustard Parsnips and Onions, 77
Scones, Apple-Cinnamon, *228*, 229–30
Shellfish. *See* Shrimp
Shrimp
  Cauliflower Rice Paella, 136–38, *137*
  Grain-Free Crispy Honey, and Bok Choy, 131–32, *133*
  Pesto, and Cauli Puree, 172, *173*
  and Shishitos, *94*, 95
Smoked Salmon Toasts with Crème Fraîche, 245
Smoothie, Matcha-Kale, 101
Smoothie Packs, Orange-Ginger, 46, *47*
Soups
  Black Bean, 126, *127*
  Chicken Tikka Masala, *188*, 189–90
  Summer Corn Chowder, *122*, 123–24
  Tomato and Red Pepper, *198*, 199

Spice Blend, Chai, 16, *17*
Spinach
  Chipotle Potato Pancake Stacks, *210*, 211
  Sautéed, and Dill, Pan-Seared Salmon with, 168, *169*
Squash
  Butternut, and Carnitas Tacos, *206*, 207
  Butternut, and Pancetta Risotto, 196, *197*
  Butternut, Pork and Maple, 98–100, *99*
  Sheet Pan Harissa Chicken and Veggies, 84, *85*
  Spaghetti, Pizza, *62*, 63
Sriracha
  Mayo, 149–50, *151*
  Salmon and Broccoli, 67
Sticky ingredients, measuring, 10
Strawberry
  -Balsamic Beef Medallions, 104–5, *105*
  -Feta Vinaigrette, *30*, 31
Sweet Potato(es)
  Chicken and Pesto-Stuffed, *214*, 215
  Chicken Burgers, Asian, 208, *209*
  Hash Egg Cups, 50, *51*
  Nachos, 204, *205*
  and Sage Zoodle Sauce, 14, *15*
  Toast Panini, 226, *227*

Tacos
  Carnitas and Butternut Squash, *206*, 207
  Ranchero Skillet Breakfast, 120, *121*
  Salmon and Pineapple Jicama, 216, *217*
  2 A.M., 231–32, *233*
Tartar Sauce and Grain-Free Fish Sticks, *146*, 147–48
Thermometer, instant-read, 11
Toasts, Smoked Salmon, with Crème Fraîche, 245
Tomato(es)
  Black Bean Soup, 126, *127*
  Bob's Backyard Blender Salsa, *234*, 235

California Caprese, *170*, 171
Chicken and Pesto–Stuffed Sweet Potatoes, *214*, 215
Chicken Tikka Masala Soup, *188*, 189–90
-Corn Salad, Grilled Flank Steak with, 96, *97*
Drive-Through Burger Bowls, *152*, 153
Hearty Mediterranean Salad with Lemon-Dill Dressing, *48*, 49
Mexican Pizza, *246*, 247
and Red Pepper Soup, *198*, 199
Short Rib Bolognese, *194*, 195
Summer Corn Chowder, *122*, 123–24
Sun-Dried, and Goat Cheese Frittata, *134*, 135
Sweet Potato Nachos, 204, *205*
Tortillas
  Carnitas and Butternut Squash Tacos, *206*, 207
  Chorizo and Potato Enchiladas, 222–25, *223*
  Ranchero Skillet Breakfast Tacos, 120, *121*
  2 A.M. Tacos, 231–32, *233*
Tostones, Cuban Sandwich on, *218*, 219
Trifle, Ground Beef, with Cauliflower Puree, *52*, 53–54
Turkey
  Hangry Man Plate, 55–56, *57*
Tzatziki, Greek Meatballs, and Cukes, 162–64, *163*

Vegetables. *See specific vegetables*
Vinaigrette, Strawberry-Feta, *30*, 31

Watermelon
  and Halloumi Skewers, 158, *159*
  -Lime Spritzer, CBD, *248*, 249
Wine, chilling, 9

Yogurt
  Arugula Melon Prosciutto Bowls, *44*, 45
  and Caramelized Cherries, 114, *115*
  Tzatziki, 162, *163*